To my friend Ruth
with my devotion.

Roy

A STORY OF GOD'S GRACE

RUTH

CYRIL J. BARBER

A STORY OF GOD'S GRACE

RUTH

CYRIL J. BARBER

An Expositional
Commentary

LOIZEAUX BROTHERS

Neptune, New Jersey

Copyright © 1983, 1989 by Cyril J. Barber

Originally published by Moody Press, 1983.

Published by Loizeaux Brothers, Inc., a nonprofit organization devoted to the Lord's work and to the spread of his truth.

All Scripture quotations, except where noted otherwise, are the author's translation.

Library of Congress Cataloging in Publication Data

Barber, Cyril J.
    Ruth, an expositional commentary/Cyril J. Barber.
        p. cm.
    Reprint. Originally published: Chicago: Moody Press, © 1983.
    Includes bibliographical references and indexes.
    ISBN 0-87213-024-X
    1. Bible. O.T. Ruth—Commentaries. I. Title.
BS1315.3.B37 1989   89-2763
222′.3507 83-dc19   CIP

Printed in the United States of America

The Hebrew letter that encloses each chapter number is the first letter in the Hebrew spelling of Ruth.

For my dear friend and pastor,
DR. CHARLES R. SWINDOLL,
whose ministry to me through the years
has been a constant source
of encouragement and blessing

CONTENTS

ACKNOWLEDGMENTS

The author and publisher wish to express their thanks to the following publishers who have graciously given permission for the use of copyrighted material in this book:

Doubleday and Company for permission to quote from E. F. Campbell's *Ruth* (Anchor Bible).

Harper & Row, Publishers, for permission to quote from O. Eissfeldt's *The Old Testament: An Introduction.*

Harper's for permission to quote from the January 1976 issue of their magazine.

Johns Hopkins University Press for permission to quote from M. Weinfeld's article on "Ruth" in the *Encyclopedia Judaica.*

The Mack Publishing Company for permission to quote from D. A. Leggett's *Levirate and Goel Institutions in the Old Testament.*

Multnomah Press for permission to quote from C. R. Swindoll's *Make Up Your Own Mind . . . About the Issues of Life.*

Tyndale Press, London, for permission to quote from L. Morris's *Ruth* (Tyndale Old Testament Commentaries).

FOREWORD

At the foot of the gray ridge on which the city of Bethlehem was built lie the "shepherds' fields," where flocks used in the sacrifices at Jerusalem were pastured by temple shepherds. There also stood the shepherds' watchtower—the tower of the flock, or *Middol Eder*—where, according to Micah, dominion would come to the daughter of Zion (Mic. 4:8). Bethlehem was certainly the birthplace of David (1 Sam. 16), but Micah anticipated that night when the tower of the flock would be bathed in celestial light and surrounded by angelic hosts (Luke 2:9), for it was in Bethlehem that the Supreme Ruler of Israel would be born (Mic. 5:2).

One can picture the excited shepherds leaving their flocks, making their way up the terraced hill to the summit, guided only by the light of the lamp that hung from the rope across the entrance to the local inn, and finding a newborn babe in the inn's filthy courtyard. The inn has long since disappeared, but there is little doubt that the Church of the Nativity stands today upon the authentic site. The evidence of the centuries is too strong to dispute.

But centuries earlier those fields were covered with grain and were the possession of a middle-aged farmer of Bethlehem. It was in those fields that Ruth the Moabitess gleaned, and it was there on that hillside that the scenes of the most delightful idyll of the Book of Ruth occurred. Before the inn was built on the hill's summit, the house of the wealthy Boaz stood there; and before the courtyard was occupied by cattle and donkeys, the open space was a threshing floor.

It would be difficult to find a city gate in Bethlehem today, but the old city of Jerusalem provides the picture. In the open space around the inside of the gate, the commercial bargains were struck—with the same haggling and argument that still go on. Here also the old men of the city would gather to sit on the ground or on stones and discuss the problems of the day. People with difficulties sought their wisdom and brought cases to them for their discussion and decision. The passing crowds would listen to their lengthy arguments and judgments. Few would question the wisdom of the elders or their conclusions.

It is still possible to imagine the self-possessed Boaz standing among them and accosting his relative in order that his problem might be solved.

How real it all seems, yet how remote from the present day. Or is it? Dr. Cyril Barber has deftly and capably demonstrated the relevance of Ruth's story to the present day. Not only has he given us an extremely satisfying exposition of the Old Testament book, but he has deduced from it many lessons that are pertinent to us in our late twentieth century circumstances. The references in the appendix indicate the extent of his research and the breadth of his reading, and we are consequently his debtors. Here is a book that deserves to be read—and then re-read. I wholeheartedly commend it.

Frederick A. Tatford

PREFACE

In his fine treatment of the Book of Ruth, the famous Scottish preacher, Dr. William M. Taylor, related an incident from the life of Benjamin Franklin.

> It is said that Dr. Franklin was once in the company of several ladies of the English nobility when the conversation turned upon pastoral poetry. The ladies took a considerable part in the discussion, and after hearing their criticisms on various authors, the doctor offered to read the translation of a pastoral for their amusement. He read, with a few verbal alterations, the Book of Ruth. They were enraptured, pronounced it the finest they had ever heard from any language, and insisted upon knowing who had written it. Imagine their confusion when he told them that he had read it from the Bible.

The story of the Book of Ruth may be better known today, but its message still appears wrapped in obscurity. In fact, very few expositions of Ruth have been published in English in the last one hundred years, and less than a handful are worthy of a reader's time and attention.

This neglect of Ruth was brought home to me quite forcefully several years ago when the pastor of a suburban church near our home became ill. I was asked to fill the pulpit during his absence. Because I did not know how many Sundays would be involved, I chose a portion from the short Book of Ruth for each Sunday morning's exposition.

In seeking for useful exegetical and expository material, I found that the only English work to have been published in recent years had been written by the renowned Australian Bible scholar, Dr. Leon Morris (1968). Then, in the same year in which I delivered the messages on Ruth (1975), Dr. Edward F. Campbell, Jr., had his commentary published in *The Anchor Bible.*

Two other significant studies have since appeared. These are Donald A. Leggett's *The Levirate and Goel Institutions in the Old Testament* (1974)—a work that was not available to me at the time I first gave my studies on Ruth—and Jack M. Sasson's *Ruth, a New Translation with a Philological Commentary and a Formalist-Folklorist Interpretation* (1979). Both of these works were prepared as dissertations.

It is important for an expositor to be familiar with matters of criticism and interpretation. However, I also believe the Scriptures to be the inspired and inerrant Word of God to man. Many modern,

esoteric approaches to the text detract from the theme of a book
and leave the needy searcher bereft of spiritual nourishment, counsel, and direction. It has therefore been my desire to carefully study
and follow the biblical text, allowing its teachings to emerge unfet-
tered by critical assumptions.

These studies on the Book of Ruth were originally published in
two magazines, one domestic and the other foreign. Then I reworked
the material entirely for a series of weekly Bible studies given to the
library staff of the International Christian Graduate University,
California, where I happened to be serving as a consultant. These
studies were based upon the Masoretic text, and they are repro-
duced here in much the same informal manner in which they were
delivered.

Between the delivery of the expository studies in 1975 and the
leading of the informal Bible studies with the library staff of the
university, I kept returning to the theme of the Book of Ruth—a
theme that I believe reveals the grace of God in the Old Testament.
Now that my investigation in the teaching of this important portion
of God's revelation has drawn to a close, I trust that what follows
will be read with profit by all who study this brief, but important,
section of God's Word.

So as not to distract the reader, I placed critical studies and notes
in appendixes.

In publishing these studies, no claim is made for any erudition. In
preparing these messages, I endeavored to do what all preachers
and teachers do. I researched each passage as thoroughly as my
time and the reference works at my disposal would allow. Certain
books and journal articles were not available to me. I am sure that,
had I had access to these materials, the content of this slender
volume would have been much improved.

Although I freely acknowledge the benefit derived from reflecting
on what others have written, no attempt has been made to synthe-
size their exemplary studies and serve it up as if it were my own. I
regard their contribution as unique, and the worst disservice that
could be done some of the older writers would be to sully their
treatment with a superficial modern restatement. In preparing these
studies, I reflected on the central teaching of each passage and then
tried to provide those who attended the studies with something that
I hoped would be both timely and relevant. My readers will soon
sense, however, that I am more at home in a classroom than a pulpit.

Because it is important for each one of us in studying the Bible to follow the text of Scripture as closely as possible, I have supplied my own translation throughout. This may at first seem to be a pedantic exercise; however, because of the many excellent paraphrases and translations of the Bible on the market—each aiming at fluidity of style and contemporaneity of expression—I may perhaps be forgiven the literalness of my translation. There is another reason, though, why I have included my own rendering of the Hebrew text. Numerous peculiarities are to be found in the original that may not come out in a translation. These are often of great importance in understanding what God revealed, and the only way to draw attention to these nuances and idiosyncrasies in the original writer's style was through a literal translation.

Because these studies of the text and teaching of the Book of Ruth were delivered weekly, a certain amount of repetition was inevitable. I trust that my readers will pardon this seeming redundancy. It was difficult to avoid reiteration of certain truths when key thoughts and phrases continuously were encountered in the biblical text.

I would like to mention those whose helpfulness and encouragement have meant a great deal to me. First, to my dear wife, Aldyth, whose unfailing support means so much to me; second, to my good friend, Mr. John Gamble of Emerald Isle Books, Belfast, Northern Ireland, who secured for me copies of Dr. Thomas Fuller's *A Comment on Ruth* and Dr. Edward Robinson's *Biblical Researches*—works that I had been looking for on the secondhand market for more years than I care to count, and that I was able to put to good use in this study; third, to Mr. Gerald L. Gooden, at that time librarian at Biola University, who graciously made available to me the resources of his institution; fourth, to my dear friends, Mrs. Les (Ellen) Beery, Mrs. Michael (Marilyn) Moore, and Mrs. Dan (Alberta) Smith, who typed and retyped the manuscript; and finally to Dr. Frederick A. Tatford, renowned British Bible teacher, and a fellow countryman, for so graciously reading the text of this work and supplying the foreword.

To all I say a very sincere "Thank you!"

INTRODUCTION

F. F. Bruce, the renowned British Bible scholar, has appropriately observed "the Bible was never intended to be a book for scholars and specialists only. From the very beginning it was intended to be everybody's book, and that is what it continues to be."

In the books that comprise the Old and New Testaments, God has chosen to disclose himself to us and impart truths important for us to learn. His revelation has been both purposeful and progressive. Each book of the Bible, therefore, has a distinct theme, and each enlarges our understanding of his will for us (cf. Heb. 1:1–2).

The Old Testament has long been neglected. Christians have placed more emphasis on the New Testament, for in it we read of Christ and the salvation that he came to bring. We cut ourselves off from a rich storehouse of knowledge, however, if we lose sight of the Old Testament truths. As Augustine observed, "The New [Testament] is in the Old concealed; the Old is in the New revealed."

One Old Testament book that we generally know something about is the Book of Ruth. But as we mentally rehearse the facts, can we say with equal certainty that we understand the reason why God included it in the Bible? What are we to learn from this brief story? Paul wrote that "these things happened [to those living in the Old Testament times] as examples for us, . . . and were written for our instruction" (1 Cor. 10:6, 11). What timeless truths from Ruth impress us today with their importance and relevance? If the only value derived from Ruth is a better understanding of the interpersonal relationship between two women, then we have benefited from only a superficial appreciation of the contents.

HAND OF THE POTTER

The Book of Ruth has been described as a "veritable masterpiece of the storyteller's art."[1] It is complete with symmetry of form, characterization, human emotion, restraint, dignity, and a pleasing repetitive style that fits well the mannerisms of those about whom we read. The story moves easily from the small hamlet of Bethlehem, across the River Jordan to Moab, and then back to Bethlehem.

But more than geography is involved. The book is about people, their problems and personal concerns. It is also about God. The narrative is developed primarily through conversations clustered around six scenes. Each scene reflects a complicated network of human emotion.[2]

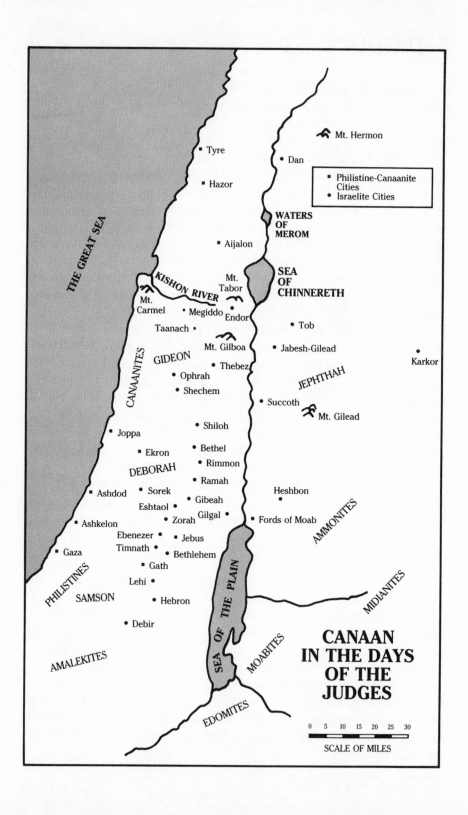

THE GREAT SEA

Mt. Hermon

■ Tyre

● Dan

■ Hazor

■ Philistine-Canaanite Cities
● Israelite Cities

■ Aijalon

WATERS OF MEROM

KISHON RIVER

Mt. Tabor

SEA OF CHINNERETH

Mt. Carmel

■ Megiddo

● Endor

● Tob

■ Taanach

Mt. Gilboa

● Jabesh-Gilead

● Karkor

CANAANITES

GIDEON

● Thebez

JEPHTHAH

● Ophrah

● Shechem

● Succoth

Mt. Gilead

● Shiloh

■ Joppa

● Bethel

■ Ekron

● Rimmon

DEBORAH

● Ramah

Heshbon
●

■ Ashdod

● Sorek

● Gibeah

AMMONITES

Eshtaol

Gilgal

● Zorah

● Fords of Moab

■ Ashkelon

Ebenezer ●

■ Jebus

Timnath ●

● Bethlehem

■ Gaza

■ Gath

Lehi ●

MIDIANITES

PHILISTINES

SEA OF THE PLAIN

SAMSON

● Hebron

● Debir

AMALEKITES

MOABITES

CANAAN IN THE DAYS OF THE JUDGES

EDOMITES

0 5 10 15 20 25 30

SCALE OF MILES

Initially, therefore, the book may be outlined as follows:

Introduction, 1:1–5
1. In Moab, 1:6–18
2. In Bethlehem, 1:19–22
3. In the Harvest Fields, 2:1–23
4. On the Threshing Floor, 3:1–18
5. Sitting in the Gate, 4:1–12
6. In the Home of Boaz, 4:13–17
   Epilogue, 4:18–22

MAIN CHARACTERS

The people also are of importance. Like the characters in a Shakespeare play, they each have an important role. They are:

Elimelech ("My God is King"), husband of Naomi.
Naomi ("Pleasant, Delightful, Lovely"), wife of Elimelech.
Mahlon ("Weakness" or "Sickness"?), son of Elimelech and Naomi, and husband of Ruth.
Chilion ("Pining" or "Consumption"?), son of Elimelech and Naomi, and husband of Orpah.
Ruth ("Friend"?), wife of Mahlon.
Orpah ("Firmness"?), wife of Chilion.
Boaz ("In Him is Strength"), a relative of Elimelech.
People of Bethlehem.
Elders of the city.
An overseer in the field.
Workers in the harvest field.
An unnamed kinsman.

AN OVERVIEW OF RUTH

Migration of the Family

The story is set in the time when the judges "judged" (i.e., governed or ruled) the tribes of Israel.[3] The writer tells about a famine that threatened the livelihood of Elimelech and his family. To save their temporal possessions, they set out for Moab (1:1–2). The initial stay in Moab soon takes on the nature of settled residency. Furthermore, Elimelech dies, leaving Naomi a widow with two sons (v. 3).

These two sons, Mahlon and Chilion, marry Moabite women, Ruth and Orpah, and reside in the land for about ten years. Each couple, however, remains childless. When Mahlon and Chilion also die, the three widows are left desolate and destitute (1:4–5).

Naomi determines to return to Judah because she can no longer live and maintain herself respectably in a foreign land. Her sorrowing daughters-in-law accompany her. Naomi, however, senses the impracticality of their decision and, in an impassioned and noble statement, insists that they each return to their mother's home (1:8–13). Orpah relents, but Ruth refuses to heed Naomi's remonstrance (1:14). James Morison paraphrased Ruth's words to Naomi as follows:

> Insist not on me forsaking thee,
> To return from following after thee:
> For whither thou goest, I will go;
> And wheresoever thou lodgest, I will lodge:
> Thy people [will be] my people,
> And thy God [will be] my God;
> Wheresoever thou diest, I will die,
> And there will I be buried.
> So may *Yahweh* do to me,
> And still more,
> If aught but death part thee and me
> (1:16–17).[4]

So Ruth accompanies Naomi to Bethlehem. These two widows, the one old and beyond the age of bearing children and the other young and in the prime of life, face a bleak future, but their hearts have been knit together in mutual affection, and as we shall see, each will look out for the other.

When Naomi and Ruth, travel-worn and weary, enter the small village of Bethlehem, the women come out to see them. Faintly recognizing Naomi after an absence of ten years, they exclaim, "Is this Naomi?" The recollection of the meaning of her name causes Naomi to say with pain and sadness of heart, "Do not call me Naomi [meaning 'pleasantness'] but call me Mara [meaning 'bitterness'] for *Shaddai* ['the Almighty'] has dealt bitterly with me" (1:18–21).

God in his grace, however, brings Naomi and Ruth back to Judah at the beginning of the barley harvest. They will not be destitute (1:22).

OLD TESTAMENT BIBLE CHRONOLOGY

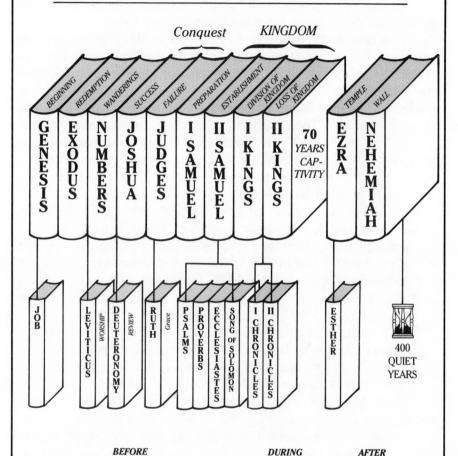

Conquest   *KINGDOM*

BEGINNING · REDEMPTION · WANDERINGS · SUCCESS · FAILURE · PREPARATION · ESTABLISHMENT · DIVISION OF KINGDOM · LOSS OF KINGDOM · TEMPLE · WALL

GENESIS · **EXODUS** · **NUMBERS** · **JOSHUA** · **JUDGES** · **I SAMUEL** · **II SAMUEL** · **I KINGS** · **II KINGS** · **70 YEARS CAP-TIVITY** · **EZRA** · **NEHEMIAH**

JOB

LEVITICUS *WORSHIP* · DEUTERONOMY *REVIEW* · RUTH *Grace* · PSALMS · PROVERBS · ECCLESIASTES · SONG OF SOLOMON · I CHRONICLES · II CHRONICLES

ESTHER

400 QUIET YEARS

BEFORE CAPTIVITY			DURING CAPTIVITY	AFTER CAPTIVITY
ISAIAH	JOEL	MICAH	EZEKIEL	HAGGAI
JEREMIAH	AMOS	NAHUM	DANIEL	ZECHARIAH
LAMENTATIONS	OBADIAH	HABAKKUK		MALACHI
HOSEA	JONAH	ZEPHANIAH		

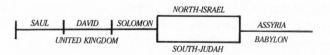

SAUL | DAVID | SOLOMON   NORTH-ISRAEL   ASSYRIA

UNITED KINGDOM   SOUTH-JUDAH   BABYLON

—H. G. Hendricks

Provision for the Family

With hunger a gnawing reality, Ruth asks Naomi for permission to glean what the reapers have left behind in the fields. In the providence of God Ruth "happens" to choose a section of the field belonging to Boaz. She knows nothing of his relationship to her late father-in-law and asks the overseer only for permission to glean in the field (2:1–3).

Shortly before midday, Boaz comes from the city and greets the reapers cordially. Then, noticing a stranger, he inquires, "Whose young woman is this?" The overseer informs him, and Boaz instructs the workers to treat her with courtesy and respect. He also speaks to Ruth and encourages her. Later, at the noon meal, he invites her to join him (2:4–16).

Ruth labors all day and at sunset threshes the grain from the husks. She then takes what she has gleaned, together with some of her leftovers from lunch, and returns to Naomi. Naomi's hunger is such that she does not inquire of Ruth how matters went until after she has eaten. Then, when she hears that it was in Boaz's field that Ruth has gleaned, she says, "This man is our relative; [in fact] he is one of our closest relatives" (2:17–23).

Ruth continues to glean in the fields of Boaz until the end of the wheat harvest. When the winnowing of the grain begins, Naomi suggests to Ruth that she ask Boaz to marry her. The provision for such a union had been established in antiquity (cf. Gen. 38) and was a part of the Scriptural tradition of God's ancient people Israel (Deut. 25:5–10).

Ruth accedes to Naomi's plan (3:1–5). She goes down to the threshing floor and takes note of the place where Boaz lies down for the night. When all is quiet and the men are evidently asleep, Ruth goes and lies down at his feet. During the night, when Boaz moves, he senses that somebody is with him. He inquires who it is and Ruth identifies herself. She then requests that Boaz fulfill the obligations of a kinsman by marrying her (3:6–9).

Boaz is moved by Ruth's loyalty to the traditions of his people and her desire to care for Naomi by marrying someone from within the family, and he praises her. He also assures her that he will do as she has requested, but he informs her that there is a relative nearer of kin to Elimelech than he, and that this relative has the right of first refusal (3:10–12).

Ruth remains on the threshing floor with Boaz until the darkness begins to fade with the approaching dawn. Boaz then sends her back to Naomi with six measures of barley as a token of his intention to fulfill his word (3:13–18).

Redemption of the Family

Early in the morning, Boaz takes his place at the gate of the city. When the man who is nearer of kin passes by, Boaz calls to him. The words *"pelonî 'almonî,"* inform the kinsman that Boaz has a legal matter to transact with him.

Boaz then impanels ten of the most trustworthy elders of the city and advises Naomi's kinsman that Elimelech's widow on account of her poverty is compelled to sell the piece of land that formerly belonged to her husband. Boaz then begins to press home his point by recommending that this relative buy the land from Naomi. If he should not wish to do so, Boaz will perform the duty of kinsman. Boaz's relative ignores the offer and expresses his willingness to buy the land (4:2–4).

But Boaz is not finished. He informs his unnamed relative:

> On the day you buy the field from the hand of Naomi, you must also acquire Ruth the Moabitess, the widow of the deceased, in order to raise up the name of the deceased on his inheritance (4:5).

The anonymous kinsman under these additional stipulations is now unwilling to take Ruth and Naomi into his home and declines to accept the terms. He then takes off his shoe and gives it to Boaz, symbolically transferring to him the right to plant his foot (i.e., take possession of) on all that was his by right (4:1–8).

From this point onward the story hastens toward its conclusion. In the presence of those gathered to witness the transaction, Boaz states that he not only buys Naomi's land but also takes Ruth to be his wife (4:9–12). The elders of the city and the people pronounce a benediction on Boaz:

> May *Yahweh* make the woman who is coming into your home like Rachel and Leah, both of whom built the house of Israel; and may you achieve wealth in Ephrathah and become famous in Bethlehem. Moreover, may your house be like the house of Perez whom Tamar bore to Judah, through the offspring that the Lord shall give you by this young woman (4:11–12).

The Lord enables Ruth to conceive, and she bears a son (4:13–17). He is called Obed (meaning "servant").

The story closes by bringing to the attention of the reader two important facts: (1) The Lord fully compensates Naomi for the loss of her husband and sons (4:15–17); and (2) Ruth becomes, unknown to her, the great-grandmother of King David (4:18–22), and stands in the ancestral line of the Lord Jesus Christ (Matt. 1:5).

1 THE DYNAMICS OF LIFE'S DECISIONS

Ruth
1:1–5

Making decisions is a complicated process. Some of the decisions we make are practical, others are theoretical; some are thrust on us from without, others we arrive at ourselves; some are of little consequence, but others are far-reaching in their importance.

The whole decision-making process has been made even more complicated for us by the world in which we live. A high premium has been placed on being "successful," and only the "right" decisions can be expected to meet with approval. Even in Christian circles, a decision will rarely be questioned if the ends achieved appear to further the work we are doing.

Life, therefore, and the whole decision-making process, have come to resemble a maze. Our desire for approval, when mingled with our beliefs and values, hedges decisions with doubt and uncertainty. How then are we to know what to do? Whose counsel can we trust? The views of those around us are often contradictory.

Many people wish that they could make decisions with the ease of James Thurber's fictional character Walter Mitty. A timid and retiring kind of person, Walter Mitty possessed a vivid imagination. He imagined himself to be fearless and resolute and possessed of the ability to immediately size up a situation and make the right decision. In this he shared a great deal in common with us in our fantasies or daydreams.

When driving his wife to the hairdresser one afternoon, Mitty imagined himself the commander of a plane carrying vital supplies. The situation was tense. A hurricane was brewing. The crew was scared, yet the supplies had to be delivered. Only he had the ability to make the split-second decisions that would enable him to pilot the plane through such weather.

"Not so fast! You're driving too fast!" says Mrs. Mitty.

"Hmm?" says Mitty, looking at his wife absent-mindedly, while the roar of the imagined aircraft faded into the remote recesses of his mind.

After dropping off his wife at the hairdresser's, Mitty drove aimlessly around. He passed the hospital. Once more he was transported in his imagination into a tense and difficult situation. He was in an operating room.

"It's the millionaire banker, Wellington McMillan," whispers a pretty nurse.

"Yes," says Dr. Mitty. "Who has the case?"

"Dr. Renshaw and Dr. Benbow, but there are two specialists here, Dr. Remington from New York and Mr. Pritchard-Mitford from London."

The patient, however, is dying.

"Coreopsis has set in," says Dr. Renshaw with a note of mingled resignation and despair in his voice. "If you would take over, Mitty?"

"If you wish."

And once again, through his ability to size up a situation and make the right decision, Walter Mitty succeeded where others would only have failed.[1]

SOURCE OF TENSION

In contrast to Walter Mitty, we make real-life decisions. Because decisions have such a far-reaching effect on our lives, we need to understand clearly the dynamics of decision making.

Decisions are reached when external and internal stimuli prompt us to action. We receive different kinds of data via our senses. This information triggers our thought processes. The information is filtered through our memories and integrated with our past experiences and the things we have learned. The emotional side of our natures also swings into action and provides us with either affirmation or a note of alarm. Based on the information supplied by both our minds and emotions, our wills are motivated to action.

RUTH 1:1–5

A CASE IN POINT

In the first chapter of Ruth, we have a whole range of decisions. Elimelech was faced with the prospect of economic ruin. He chose to go to Moab and took his wife and two children.

Although we will look specifically at the case of Elimelech, his decision was not the only one in this chapter worthy of consideration. In Moab, Elimelech died. Naomi, his wife, decided to remain in Moab, and there, far removed from the comfort of friends and relatives, adjusted to the problems of widowhood.

While in Moab, Elimelech's two sons, Mahlon and Chilion, decided to marry. From the order of their wives' names, it would seem as if the elder, Mahlon, married Ruth (4:10) *after* his younger brother had first married Orpah (note 1:4 where Ruth was spoken of as the "second" of the wives of Elimelech's sons).

The family farmed the land for a period of about ten years. Then Mahlon and Chilion also died. Naomi's thoughts now turned homeward but not before she heard that the Lord had once again brought prosperity to her people.

When Naomi shared her decision with her daughters-in-law, Ruth and Orpah decided to accompany her. En route to the River Jordan, Naomi tried hard to dissuade them from returning to Judah with her. Her situation was hopeless. Their choice to go with her was much appreciated, but it was impractical and would only bring hardship on them. Orpah was persuaded by Naomi's words and turned back, but Ruth persisted in her determination to go with Naomi to Bethlehem.

In each of these decisions external and internal factors played an important part. Each situation permits us to observe the manner in which external stimuli (famine, death, marriage, etc.) set in motion each person's thought processes, and how this information was integrated with that person's perceptions and beliefs on the one hand, and feelings and desires (or drives) on the other. The result in each case was a decision that was in keeping with that individual's true nature.

ERA OF DISCONTENT

We notice first in the biblical narrative all the external pressures that give rise to decisions. The story of Ruth begins with the word

RUTH 1:1–5

and[2] thereby placing the events that are recorded in the mainstream of God's revelatory history.

> And it came to pass [lit., "and it was"] in the days when the judges governed, that there was a famine in the land. And a [certain] man from Bethlehem in Judah [lit., Bethlehem-Judah] went to sojourn in the fields of Moab, he and his wife, and his two sons. And the name of the man [was] Elimelech, and the name of his wife, Naomi; and the name[s] of his two sons, Mahlon and Chilion, Ephrathites of Bethlehem in Judah. And they came to the fields of Moab and stayed there. And Elimelech, Naomi's husband, died; and she was left, she and her two sons. And they took to themselves [as] wives women of Moab; the name of the one [was] Orpah, and the name of the other [lit., second], Ruth; and they lived there about ten years. Then Mahlon and Chilion also died, both of them, and the woman was bereft [lit., left] of her two children and her husband (1:1–5).

With simple brevity the writer began his story with a period of Israel's history when judges "judged" God's people (Judg. 19:1, 21:25). No established government existed in those days. Everyone did what was right in his own eyes. It was an era in which history was continuously repeating itself. Following a time of walking in submission to the revealed will of God, the people would "do evil in his sight." They would apostatize and serve the licentious gods of the heathen nations about them. To chasten them, the Lord would allow the nations whose gods they were worshipping to oppress them. This would cause the Israelites great economic and emotional distress. In their plight, they would repent and turn back to the Lord. He would then raise up a judge to deliver them. They would enjoy the blessing of the Lord during the remainder of the judge's lifetime. But on his death they would again turn their backs on the Lord with the result that the cycle would begin all over again (cf. Judg. 2:11–3:11; etc.).

PERSONAL REMINISCENCES

The Book of Ruth passes from the oppression and strife of the period of the judges to the quiet, domestic life of a family in Judah. It moves from the din of battle to a humble cottage in Bethlehem.[3] Through an ordinary family, the writer of Ruth explained old customs as well as the pressure of unexpected events. He showed the toiling sheepherder, and later on, the busy reapers. He helped the reader to sense their cares, witness the devotion of women to their husbands, and experience with them their sorrows. He began at a time in their history when a famine swept over the land. Such occurrences were not uncommon. Earlier famines had caused Abraham (Gen. 12) and Jacob (Gen. 41–46) to go down to Egypt and Isaac (Gen. 26) to take refuge in Philistia.

God in his sovereignty had promised his people Israel that, if they walked in his ways, he would prosper them in all areas of life (cf. Deut. 28:1–4). On the other hand, if they rebelled against him and did not obey his word, he assured them that he would chasten them (28:15–68). One of the means he might choose to use in disciplining their waywardness was famine[4] (Lev. 26:16, 21; Deut. 11:16–17; Ps. 105:16; Lam. 4:4–6; Ezek. 14:21; etc.).

It is significant that the famine we read about in Ruth 1 extended over all the land. Even the little village of Bethlehem in Judah was affected.

Bethlehem lay on a narrow ridge about six miles south of Jerusalem. It occupied a spur of the central mountain range that projects eastward away from the main ridge. From this favored position, the terraced slopes broke away sharply to fertile fields on the north, east, and south. The terraces were admirably suited to the growth of olive and fig trees and the cultivation of vines. The valleys below were ideal for wheat and barley, and hillsides farther from the village had been used for the grazing of flocks and herds from time immemorial. Such was the fertility of the region that Bethlehem, ancient Ephrathah, was called "the Granary" (Heb., "House of Bread").

MISCALCULATION

With this historic background before us, we come to consider Elimelech's resolve to go to Moab. From his experiences, we learn something of the internal dynamics that prompt our decisions.

The famine in Canaan is so severe that Elimelech (*Eli,* "my God"; [is] *melek,* "king") feels compelled to leave his lands and with his surviving livestock and his family seeks to preserve his remaining wealth by immigrating for a time into Moab.

Farmers are usually very attached to the soil, and Elimelech must have chosen to leave Judah for Moab as only a last resort.

But why go to Moab? Why not Egypt or Philistia?

During the period of the judges, Israel was continuously at war with the Philistines. Going there would obviously be out of the question. And because Philistia's border flanked the road leading to Egypt, some writers have conjectured that they harassed those Israelites who chose to make the journey to the Land of the Nile.

It seems probable, therefore, that as Elimelech sees the sheep dying in the parched valleys and hears the mournful lowing of the now gaunt cattle (i.e., the external data received via his senses), he feels a sense of desperation grip him (i.e., his internal response).[5] For months he has hoped for some token that the famine will soon be over, but none has appeared. He has scanned the Jordan valley, but it, too, lies barren beneath the baking rays of the sun. But there, in the distance, he can see that the hills of Moab are tinged with green.

When Elimelech can tolerate the situation no longer, he decides to take his remaining cattle and his few surviving sheep to Moab. His decision is reached only after careful deliberation. Safeguards are built into it:

- He and his family will go to Moab as resident aliens (this is inherent in the Hebrew word *gûr,* 1:1, translated "to live" in most versions). They will not identify themselves with the people of Moab (something that would be expected of someone taking up permanent residence there).
- He will seek to avoid the contamination of the idolatrous practices of the Moabites by sojourning in the fields,[6] not residing in any of the cities.
- The stay in Moab will be temporary, just long enough to survive the effects of the famine in Judah.

But why, we may ask, was Elimelech so concerned about going to another land when others were not? The answer is most revealing. The text informs us that Elimelech was an Ephrathite.[7] Ephrathah was the ancient name of the district in which Bethlehem stood (see Gen. 35:19; 48:7; Ruth 4:11; Mic. 5:2 [Heb. 5:1]). To be born an Ephrathite meant that Elimelech was of ancient and noble lineage. It was the equivalent of someone today coming from a well-established family in Boston, or being a third-generation resident of Charleston, South Carolina. By referring to Elimelech as an Ephrathite, the writer intended us to understand that he came from a distinguished family. He was used to being looked up to and respected in the community. He probably was also accustomed to wealth and therefore less likely

RUTH 1:1–5

to be able to withstand its loss. Fear of losing his wealth and its imagined influence in the community may have been the powerful motivating force behind his decision to sojourn in Moab.

In this connection Elimelech found himself in a situation similar to many today. For a variety of reasons such as job change or family matters, we may move to another part of the country. Before we relocate, we must face the issues of finding a place to stay, ascertaining the spiritual climate of our new surroundings, and considering its effect on our children and even whom they will marry. Because of these issues and how they affect others, we must carefully make our decisions.

GRAVEN IMAGES

In Elimelech's case, the people involved in his decision include his wife, Naomi (whose name, as mentioned previously, probably signifies "pleasant [one]," "lovely," "delightful"), and their two sons, Mahlon (a name possibly derived from the Hebrew root meaning "to be weak") and Chilion (a name that may signify to be of "failing" [health], or "pining").[8] These names all appeared in other literature of this period (specifically ancient Ugaritic texts from Ras Shamra).

Apparently Elimelech's household is in basic agreement with his plan. They do not seem to be concerned about residing for a while among the descendants of Abraham's nephew, Lot. The language of the Moabites is similar to Hebrew; and by choosing to live in the "fields of Moab," they will be associating with people whose interests in farming and animal husbandry are similar to their own.

Moab was only about forty to sixty miles from Bethlehem, depending on the route taken. The closest and most easily accessible part of Moab to emigrants from Bethlehem would be the northern portion. Moab lay north of the River Arnon (modern Wadi Mojib) and extended to a line adjacent to the upper end of the Dead Sea. This section was approximately 3,700 feet above the level of the Dead Sea and about 2,000–2,400 feet above sea level. It was well watered and relatively flat. As such, it was ideal for farming and the raising of livestock.

Verse 2 of the narrative reveals that Elimelech and his family, after arriving in Moab, decide to *remain* there.[9] Everything is to their liking. They sense an acceptance on the part of the people who possibly help them get established. New friendships are made, and their original intent of returning to Judah as soon as possible is postponed. The biblical text is very explicit on this point, and the change in the use of verb clearly indicates a change in the original plan. This being the case, we learn from the story of Elimelech how the effects of change can subtly undermine our initial decisions.

NO HIDING PLACE

Dr. F. W. Boreham has observed that it is possible for us to "make our decisions, and then our decisions to turn around and make us." He was right. In Moab, Elimelech apparently found the people tolerant of his religious beliefs, and with many of his early concerns defused and his emotional needs so evidently fulfilled, he decided to remain there.[10]

The next event we read about is Elimelech's death. No explanation is given. Was this a judgment from God for leaving the land of his appointment?

Commentators have lined up on both sides of the issue. Dr. Samuel Cox, for example, said: "Elimelech lost his life while seeking a livelihood, and found a grave where he sought a home. And, apparently, this 'judgment' fell on him at once, judgment treading on the very heels of offense [in leaving the Land of Promise]."[11]

Thomas Fuller was inclined to attribute Elimelech's passing to natural causes rather than divine judgment. In his quaint way he pointed out:

> I have seldom seen a tree thrive that has been transplanted when it is old. The same may be seen in Elimelech; his aged body brooks not the foreign air; though he could avoid the arrows of famine in Israel, yet he could not shun the darts of death in Moab; he that lived in a place of penury, must die in a land of plenty. Let none condemn Elimelech's removal as unlawful, because of his sudden death; for those actions are not ungodly which are unsuccessful, nor those pious which are prosperous; seeing the lawfulness of an action is not to be gathered from the joyfulness of the event, but from the justness of the cause, for which it is undertaken.[12]

We should be cautious in applying either censure or praise where Scripture is silent. But Elimelech's sudden passing, so soon after his change in plans, does seem to indicate that evidence of God's intervention may not be altogether wanting.

The effect of Elimelech's passing on the family was that Naomi was left without the protection and companionship of her husband,

and her two sons were deprived of the counsel and guidance of their father. All of this brings us to consider the outcome of decision making.

SIGNIFICANT CONSEQUENCES

Following the death of Elimelech,[13] Naomi decides to remain in Moab. She apparently shares the same values as her husband and fears the loss of her earthly possessions if she returns to Judah.

In time Naomi's sons, having assumed the responsibilities for running the farm, decide to add to their emblems of manhood. Each marries a Moabite girl. Mahlon's wife is named Ruth (a name that may mean "friendship"),[14] and Chilion's is called Orpah (a word that may be derived from *'orep,* "neck").[15] The text states emphatically, "and they stayed there about ten years" (1:4). Apparently neither of them wanted to return to their homeland.

But what are we to understand by these marriages? Was it right for these Israelites to marry Moabites? Did Naomi try to dissuade them from marrying outside of their tribe?

One of the Jewish Targums said that Mahlon and Chilion "transgressed the commandment of the Lord, and took foreign wives from among the daughters of Moab." Many of the older commentators, drawing mistakenly on Deuteronomy 23:3, are loud in denouncing the sins of Naomi's sons. In fairness, this verse does not prohibit marriage to Moabites (as Deut. 7:1–5 does with the inhabitants of Canaan), but only lays certain restrictions on the children of such a union.

Of far greater importance in our consideration of the wider issue of marriage is the apostle Paul's warning in 2 Corinthians 6:14 about being unequally yoked together with unbelievers. In the case of Mahlon and Chilion, we have no sure knowledge that their belief in *Yahweh,* the God of Israel, went any deeper than mental assent.

But what of Naomi? How did she view the marriage of her sons to those who stood apart from the covenants of her people?

Whatever may have been her reaction and however she may have tried to dissuade them from marrying Moabite women, she must have accepted what she could not change. She became to her daughters-in-law the best mother-in-law they could ever have. And so the family, now augmented by two new brides, lives contentedly in Moab for about ten years.

RUTH 1:1–5

The text then goes on to say, "And they also died, both of them, Mahlon and Chilion, and Naomi was bereft of her two children and her husband" (v. 5).

Two more graves are now dug alongside the one holding the remains of Elimelech. The cause of these deaths is not given, and for the purpose of the story it is unimportant. The Talmud regarded the passing of Naomi's sons as punishment for leaving Judah.[16] It is sufficient for our purpose to visualize three grieving widows, one old and two young, standing beside three graves.

We now need to concentrate our attention on several life-related lessons (or principles) in the first five verses of Ruth.

FREEDOM TO CHOOSE

One of the most prominent of these principles concerns the grace of God in allowing us freedom of choice. His relationship with us is not that of a despot. He is glorified when we make decisions in accordance with his revealed will. He realizes that we are not all alike and builds flexibility into the way in which he deals with us. He even permits us to make certain plans and try them out.[17] This is one of the ways in which we learn and come eventually to approve wholeheartedly the wisdom of his will for us (cf. Rom. 12:2).

Such decisions, of course, necessitate that we study God's Word and make its principles the basis of our actions. In this respect, we are in a more privileged position than was Elimelech or Naomi or their sons. Only the writings of Moses and the Book of Joshua (and perhaps the Book of Job) were a part of their Scriptural heritage at this time. They did not possess copies of God's Word, so they could not read it for themselves in their cottage in Bethlehem after the work of the day had been done. They were dependent on the minis-try of the priests, and if the priesthood was apostate (as it often was during the days of the judges), the Word of the Lord was not taught (cf. 1 Sam. 3:1*b*; see also 2:12ff.).

Although God's Word specifically states that Canaan was the place of his choosing for his people,[18] he allowed Elimelech freedom to make certain decisions. Elimelech was certainly aware of the history of his people and of their inheritance of the land, and that is why he built safeguards into his plan to go to Moab. Yet sadly these safeguards did not take into account the weaknesses of human na-ture. The Moabites accepted the family and tolerated their beliefs.

That led to a change in their original decision, and that change evidently moved Elimelech outside the will of God.

BETTER THAN A NAME

But what should Elimelech have done? Remain in Judah? Admittedly Judah was the place of God's appointment for Elimelech and his family. But it is too simplistic for us to say that they should have stayed in Bethlehem unless we also provide a solution to the fear that drove him to seek refuge in Moab. To biblically pontificate a course of action to Elimelech ignores the inner reason behind Elimelech's decision. We, therefore, place ourselves on a par with Job's comforters if we do not provide Elimelech with something strong enough to overcome his fears (see 1 Cor. 10:13).

A close examination of the passage indicates that Elimelech attributed to the famine two characteristics that properly belong to God: almightiness (the power to take away his autonomy) and impendency (the power to do him harm). In Elimelech's case, the famine threatened his well-being, his family's, and had the potential of robbing him of his position in the community. The famine was a fear-object.[19] It generated within him a fear-conflict between what he knew to be right (i.e., remaining in the land) and the possibility of preserving his possessions by going to Moab. If he was successful, he could later return to Judah with his prosperity intact and be more influential than ever before.

In thinking as he did, Elimelech made the mistake of equating wealth with influence. But deciding to go to Moab did not put an end to Elimelech's fears. He knew that the Moabites were a sinful people. This generated further internal conflict, and this new source of tension was only resolved when he decided to compromise. He would avoid the cities (which had been Lot's worst mistake, Gen. 13:5–13; 19:1ff.) and live instead in the "fields of Moab." With this safeguard built into his plan, he was able to overcome his fear-conflicts.

Yet Elimelech carried about with him a testimony to the power of God. This had been given to him by his parents. His name signified "My God is King." Yet he failed to acknowledge God's sovereignty in the famine and did not live in submission to his will.

Did he doubt God's power and concern for him? This is often the mistake we make, and it may have been Elimelech's as well. When we think this way, we fail to give the Lord the supreme position in our lives. When we do acknowledge him to be the Lord of our lives, we are able to commit ourselves and our temporal circumstances to him and trust ourselves to his wise care.

The name that we bear as Christians (i.e., "Christ's ones") is more than an empty term. It should indicate the reality of a dynamic relationship with him and of our confidence in him.

Before leaving these fascinating verses, we must also consider carefully the effect of our decisions on others.

SWORD OF DAMOCLES

No matter how careful we are in making decisions and reaching conclusions, a "sword of Damocles" hangs over our heads. Someone either known to us or unknown may adversely be affected by what we do.

Fortunately for us, God's Word has some helpful counsel. The apostle Paul gave some to the believers in Corinth.[20] Basically, he said this: We need to constantly keep in mind the influence of our attitudes and conduct on others. We may engage in practices that for us are quite legitimate, yet these may cause a person of lesser maturity than ourselves to "stumble." In the exercise of our liberty, therefore, we should always be motivated by true *agapē* love (the desire for the highest good for the one loved, even to the point of self-sacrifice).

These principles from Ruth 1:1–5, so simple yet so important, can prevent our ulterior motives from (1) coloring our actions; (2) distorting our decisions; and (3) unwittingly involving others in the consequences of our deeds.

RUTH 1:1–5

2 | THE PURPOSE OF GOD IN HUMAN SUFFERING

Ruth
1:6–22

Psychologists tell us that there are two primary relational emotions: love and fear. Of these, love is the positive emotion and has the power to overcome fear (1 John 4:8).

Love, as we see it develop in our children, progresses through four distinct stages.[1] Initially, as infants, our children feel loved when their basic needs are met. As long as they are warm, clean, and well fed, they are content. They are the center of their own little universe, and everything revolves around them.

Then, as our children grow older and are able to move about for themselves, restrictions are placed on them—what they can and cannot do. At this stage, they interpret love as being left alone to do what they want.

Within a few years, their sense of being loved stems from the compliments people pay them, the gifts they receive, and the ways in which they are made to feel special. This phase of their development may last well into their teen years, perhaps even for life. Included in the more advanced part of this stage is the emergence of romantic attachment toward someone else. During these years of development, they feel loved when someone else is giving them their undivided attention, but self is still prominent. Love to them is very much a case of their desires being fulfilled, their needs being met, their plans succeeding, and their goals being attained.

Those desiring confirmation of the accuracy of this observation need only to spend a little time analyzing the contents of the top ten best sellers of the book industry and the leading movies being released. This will provide ample confirmation of the shallowness and self-centeredness of what is currently described as love.

Because of limited models of true love in many homes and inadequate examples of love portrayed via the media, it is no wonder that many of our children never progress to the highest stage of love. In this stage their highest delight is derived from giving of themselves in the service of others. True love may best be described as "desiring the greatest good in the one loved, even to the point of self-sacrifice."[2]

But someone may well ask, "What does all this have to do with the Book of Ruth?" The evidence of different emotions, including love, is very prominent in chapter 1. There was Naomi's love for her daughters-in-law and their love for her. There was her strong insistence that they not accompany her to Judah and their different responses. Orpah, who loved Naomi dearly, nevertheless showed that her devotion to her mother-in-law was not to be at the expense of herself and what seemed best for her future. Ruth, on the other hand, loved Naomi in a self-sacrificing way and refused to be dissuaded from returning to Bethlehem with her.

RIGHT TURN ON RED

As we consider the events described in Ruth 1:6–22 and the attitudes they disclose, we are compelled to study the experiences of those involved in the context of what had so recently taken place in their lives. Naomi, Orpah, and Ruth had suffered the loss of all they held dear. Death had taken their loved ones from them. With hearts so heavy that they felt they could no longer bear the pain, they had returned from the graveside.[3]

The plight of a widow in these times was precarious. Young widows might stay in their father's home (cf. Gen. 38:11), but an older widow whose parents were dead was dependent on her children for support. If they had already died, then her situation was precarious indeed. Unless she had the benefits of wealth left her by her late husband, she was destitute. Only in marriage was there any hope of security and the possibility of a meaningful future.

CHANGING FOR TOMORROW

With these thoughts in mind, we are ready to consider the section before us. We read:

RUTH 1:6–22

And Naomi arose, she and her daughters-in-law, and returned from the fields of Moab, for she had heard in the fields of Moab that *Yahweh* had visited his people[4] to give them bread [i.e., food]. And she went out from the place where she had been, and her two daughters-in-law with her; and they went in the way to return to the land of Judah. And Naomi said to her two daughters-in-law, "Go, return, each [of you] to the house of your mother.[5] May *Yahweh* deal kindly[6] with you[7] as you have done with the dead and with me. May *Yahweh* grant that you may find rest[8] each in the house of her husband." Then she kissed them, and they lifted up their voice[s] and wept (1:6–9).

The scene described by the writer touches our emotions. The situation of the three widows is hopeless. In the extremity of her sorrow, Naomi finds that her thoughts turn Godward and homeward (1:6; see also 13*b*, 21). She has heard in Moab that *Yahweh,* the covenant-keeping God of Israel, has visited his people once again restoring prosperity to the land. Furthermore, her presence in Moab is preventing Orpah and Ruth from returning to their homes where hopefully their fathers or mothers will arrange suitable marriages for them.

Naomi, therefore, decides to return to Judah. She has perceived the loss, first of her husband, and now of her sons, as a divine rebuke (cf. 1:13*b*). She is beginning to see God's hand in her misfortunes. She can readily discern his kindness to her people in giving them renewed prosperity. She realizes now that it was wrong for her and Elimelech to try to escape the chastening of the Lord by leaving Judah (see 1:20*b*). As the thought of returning to the place of God's appointment takes root in her mind, we see the beginning of a work of grace being done in her heart. Naomi's thoughts are now occupied with God, she sees his hand in the circumstances of life, and she feels impelled by an inner urge to go back to Bethlehem.

Naomi prepares to leave, and Orpah and Ruth accompany her. Whether Naomi communicated her intention to her daughters-in-law or whether they realized what she planned to do when they saw her place her few earthly belongings in a shawl, we have no way of knowing. Those who suffer often empathize with each other, and at such times words are unnecessary. It is probable that, out of compassion for Naomi, Orpah and Ruth decide to accompany her to Judah.

As the three of them leave the place where they have been staying and Naomi takes the path that will lead to the River Jordan, she apparently is unaware of their intention to accompany her all the way to Judah. She probably surmises that they will walk along the path with her for a short distance before engaging in one last fond farewell.

When the three widows reach some convenient place (perhaps the boundary of a field or the ford of a river), Naomi stops. She turns to her two daughters-in-law who have shared her home for the past ten years and, acknowledging their devotion to her as well as to her sons, entreats them to return each to the "house of your mother."[9] Then she prays that the Lord will bestow his grace on them even in Moab: "May *Yahweh* deal in loving-kindness with you, as you have dealt with the dead and with me" (1:8*b*).

The word that Naomi used to describe the one who will grant them his blessing (*Yahweh* as opposed to *Elohim*) immediately alerts us to God's work of grace in her heart. Realizing that true blessing comes only from him, Naomi invokes his favor on Orpah and Ruth.

The exact nature of the blessing Naomi desired for her daughters-in-law was described as *menûḥâ* "rest." It signified more than cessation of worry or anxiety. *Menûḥâ* combined the idea of security as well as blessing (cf. Josh. 21:44 where this same word was used, only in a different setting). In Naomi's prayer, *menûḥâ* implied more than marriage. It looked at the love of a husband, the comfort and security of the home he would provide, and the provision of those temporal blessings that kept one's anxieties manageable.

A POINT TO PONDER

As we again look at Naomi's words to her daughters-in-law, we notice how, in a subtle way, she permits us to glimpse the kind of relationship that existed between her and Orpah and Ruth. The use of the word *ḥeseḏ*, "loving-kindness," signified the tender, compassionate, loyal attitude of each to the other.[10] Notice the word *as* in verse 8*b*. "May *Yahweh* deal in loving-kindness with you, *as* you have dealt with the dead and with me." The loving-kindness that God showed toward his people, which also formed the basis of his relationship with them, was the same kind of attitude displayed in Naomi's family. It was no wonder that, having been surrounded by such a loving, kind atmosphere, Orpah and Ruth wished to go with Naomi to Judah.

Theologically, *ḥeseḏ* describes God's dealings with us. This is best illustrated in Exodus 34:5–8 where God described himself and explained to the assembled Israelites what they may expect from him. Through the imparting of grace, we may demonstrate the same loving concern for others. When this kind of attitude prevails in a home, then bitterness, retaliation (verbal as well as physical), criticism, and all forms of destructive conduct are excluded.

WINDS OF AUTUMN

As Orpah and Ruth hear Naomi telling them to return to their mothers' homes, they are full of sorrow. The loss of their husbands has brought calamity enough. The thought now of parting with their beloved mother-in-law is too much for them to bear. With one accord they give expression to their feelings.

The text then reveals something of Orpah's and Ruth's passionate regard for Naomi. Of their own accord and with no collusion, they say, "No,[11] we will return with you to your people."

The words are nobly spoken and their sentiment is sincere, but Naomi realizes how impossible it will be for two Moabite widows to find acceptance and any form of employment among her people. Orpah and Ruth are young and may well remarry in their own land. She is too old to still entertain the prospect of bearing children.[12] She also is in no position to provide a comfortable home for them. Naomi also knows of her people's pride of race. She knows, too, of Israel's dislike for Moabites resulting from their past association with them (cf. Num. 20:18–21, Deut. 23:4). She, therefore, lovingly, yet firmly, says to them:

> Turn back, my daughters; why should you go with me? Have I still sons in my womb that they should be [to] you for husbands? Return, my daughters, go; for I am too old to be [married] to a husband. If I should say, "There is hope for me"; even [if] I should be [married] to a husband tonight, and even [if] I should bear sons;[13] would you wait for them[14] until they grow up?[15] Would you endure not to be [married] to a husband? No, my daughters, for it is much more bitter for me than [it is] for you that the hand of *Yahweh* has gone out against me[16] (1:11–13).

Some have severely criticized Naomi for suggesting that Orpah and Ruth return to Moab.[17] They have asserted that Naomi should

have constrained both her daughters-in-law to accompany her to
Judah, for there they would have come under the influence of the
truth and may even have come to believe in the one true God. To
suggest that they return to a culture permeated by paganism and
idolatry of the worst kind was surely to damn their souls to eternal
perdition.

Dr. Samuel Cox, however, has paraphrased the intent of Naomi's
words. He wrote:

> If we would understand the scene, and especially the stress laid on
> these young widows finding new husbands, we must remember that
> in the East of antiquity, as in many Eastern lands to this day, the
> position of an unmarried woman, whether maid or widow, was a very
> unhappy and perilous one. Only in the house of a husband could a
> woman be sure of respect and protection. Hence the Hebrews spoke
> of a husband's house as a woman's *"menuchah,"* or "rest"—her se-
> cure and happy asylum from servitude, neglect, license. It was an
> "asylum" of honour and freedom that Naomi desired for Orpah and
> Ruth. But as she had to explain to them, such an "asylum," while it
> would be open to them in Moab, would be fast closed against them in
> Judah. In marrying them her sons had sinned against Hebrew law.
> That sin was not likely to be repeated by Israelites living in their own
> land. Yet how is Naomi to tell them of this fatal separation between
> the two races? How is she to make these loving women aware that, if
> they carry out their resolve to go with her, they might resign all hope
> of honor and regard?
>
> She discharges her difficult task with infinite delicacy. They, of
> course, had no thought of marrying any sons that might hereafter be
> born to the widowed Naomi. Such a thought could not possibly have
> entered their minds. Why, then, does Naomi lay such emphasis on the
> utter unlikelihood of her having sons and of their waiting for them
> even if she could have them? Simply to convey to them that, if they
> went with her, *they would have no hope but in herself.* What she
> means was: "I know and love you: and, had I sons, I would take you
> with me, that in their homes you might find the asylum every woman
> needs and craves. But I have none, nor am I likely to have any, nor
> could you wait for them if I had. And, outside my household, there is
> no prospect for you; for the men of Israel may not take to wife
> daughters of Moab. Alas, it is more bitter for me to tell you this than
> for you to hear it. It is harder for me than for you that we must part.
> But the hand of the Lord has gone out against me. I have no hope for
> the future. I must walk my darkened path alone. But you, you may find

RUTH 1:6–22

an asylum with the people of your own race. *Your* future may be bright. You will at least have one another. Go, then, and return each to her mother's house."[18]

Naomi's words have a profound effect on her daughters-in-law. As the reality of the situation penetrates their thought processes, Orpah and Ruth sense more fully than before the desperate plight they are in. They also give way once more to loud weeping (1:14).

PARTING OF THE WAYS

Naomi had previously taken the initiative by kissing her daughters-in-law. Now it is Orpah who kisses Naomi. It is a kiss of farewell. Their relationship has come to an end.[19] As Dr. Robert A. Watson has pointed out, Orpah was a type of woman who was worldly-wise.[20] To her the arguments of Naomi are persuasive. She sees the future as Naomi has painted it. In Moab she has some slender hope of future happiness. On the other hand, to go with Naomi to Judah will mean only ostracism, grief, and misery. She kisses Naomi good-bye and takes the road leading to her mother's home.

When all was going well in Naomi's household, Orpah loved her kind, considerate mother-in-law. Naomi brought happiness and stability to the home. But when the strong winds of adversity removed all buffers from her, Orpah thinks solely of herself; taking the initiative, she departs.

New Values Versus Old Traditions

Although we should not reproach Orpah too much for her decision, the writer of this uniquely beautiful story used Orpah's departure to highlight the steadfast love and devotion of Ruth. Ruth does more than embrace Naomi; she clings to her (1:14*b*). Until now Ruth has stood in the shadows. Now she emerges from obscurity and reveals a love and devotion to her mother-in-law that is at once beautiful and inspiring.

As Ruth and Naomi look together at the retreating figure of Orpah, Naomi disengages Ruth's arms from around her. "Look," she says, "your sister-in-law has returned to her people and to her gods. Return after your sister-in-law" (1:15).

Naomi's words are simple and direct. Hers is a self-sacrificing love, for it is certain that, if she had thought solely of herself, she would have delighted in the company of both of her daughters-in-law. Naomi had dealt honestly with them by aptly describing the kind of situation they would face in a strange land.

But why did Naomi mention that Orpah had returned "to her gods"? Might Naomi have said this to cause Ruth to realize the spiritual realities lying latent in her own decision? Did she sense in this young woman an emerging sensitivity to spiritual things that was missing in Orpah? We cannot be sure. What is important for us to notice is that Naomi permitted each of her daughters-in-law to make her own decision. She might weigh the issues for them, but in the final analysis each acted on her own initiative.

Ruth, having before her the example of Orpah, chooses to remain with Naomi. In a spirit of true devotion, she says:

> Do not press me to leave you, to return from [following] after you; for where you go, I will go, and where you stay, I will stay; your people [shall be] my people, and your God [will be] my God. Where you die, I will die, and there I will be buried. Thus[21] may *Yahweh* do to me, and more so, if [anything but] death parts me and you (1:16–17).

Rhetoricians are unable to improve on the eloquence of Ruth's statement. With an economy of words that astounds us, she declares her loyalty to Naomi, her willingness to be numbered among Naomi's people, and her submission to Naomi's God. In a single statement, she had separated herself from her former god(s).[22] Her knowledge of *Yahweh* was not well developed but real, and she willingly acknowledged his sovereignty over her life from this moment forward.

Crucial Choice

Ruth's love for Naomi was deep and mature. It was the self-sacrificing kind that finds its highest delight in giving of itself in the service of others.[23]

From Ruth's words in 1:16–17, it is clear that God uses human suffering to bring people to a personal knowledge of his saving grace. An individual often traces his or her spiritual awakening to some form of adversity. Ruth had been awakened to spiritual realities through the death of her husband. Now, when faced with a crucial choice, she boldly declared her submission to the authority of Naomi's God. Furthermore, she did not look on Naomi's God as a tribal deity who might rule a certain territory but not another. She acknowledged his power (in the event of her breaking her promise to Naomi) wherever she might be. In addition, she did not use the general name for God, *Elohim,* but referred to him by his most revered name, *Yahweh.*

The importance of a personal decision has been underscored by Dr. Robert Watson: "In religion there is no escape from personal decision; no one can drift to salvation with companions or with a church. . . . The supreme nature of religion and its unique part in human development are seen here, that it demands high and sustained personal effort. . . ."[24]

As with many before and since, Ruth was influenced in her decision, not by smooth words or manipulative devices, but by the example and influence of another.

SENSITIVE ISSUES

The last section of this chapter is likewise brimming with evidences of God's grace. We read:

> And when Naomi saw that Ruth was determined [lit., had made herself strong, i.e., was firmly resolved] to go with her, she ceased trying to persuade her. So they went, both of them, until they came to Bethlehem. And it was, when they came to Bethlehem, that all [who were in] the city were stirred because of them. And the women said, "Is this Naomi?" And Naomi said to them, "Do not call me 'Naomi' [meaning "pleasant"], call me 'Mara' [meaning "bitter"], for *Shaddai*[25] [the Almighty] has dealt very bitterly with me. I went out full, and *Yahweh* has brought me back empty.[26] Why do you call me 'Naomi,' since *Yahweh* has witnessed against me [lit., has eyed me], and *Shaddai* has done evil to [i.e., has afflicted] me?" (1:18–21).

The Welcome

The journey back to Judah is not described. Because it would have taken two or three days and involved sleeping in a field or a cave at night, Naomi must have been glad to have Ruth with her. Although their situation was, humanly speaking, hopeless, God is the Defender of the destitute and the Helper of the poor. Now that

RUTH 1:6–22

Naomi is returning to the place of blessing, she hopes that despite indications to the contrary, he will help her.

As they near Bethlehem, the local women[27] come out to see who is climbing the slopes to their village. They recognize Naomi, and their reaction is one of delight in welcoming back an old friend.[28] As they clamor around her, showering her with questions, Naomi expresses the deep-seated hurt in her heart. She had left Bethlehem with a husband and sons. Her desire then was to preserve her material wealth. In Moab she had lost her family, and as a result life had now become empty.

At Rock Bottom

Naomi's reaction was natural. We are apt to blame God for our misfortune when we suffer. "If he is who he claims to be," we reason, "then why didn't he prevent this from happening to me?"

In Naomi's case, she was also conscious of having done wrong (cf. 1:13*b*, 20*b*, 21*b*), and she viewed the loss of her husband and sons as God's punishment of her for her sins. That was why she used the name *Shaddai*. He was all-powerful. He had done to her as he wished. Against him she was powerless.[29]

At times like this, we may not understand the purpose God may have for our suffering. We see the grace of God at work in restoring Naomi's sense of values. In her own words, "I went out full." She had left Judah to preserve what she valued most. In Moab she had lost her husband and her sons, and with their passing, she realized life's true values. She had not realized how really blessed she was in Bethlehem, even with the famine and the threatened loss of earthly possessions. Now her system of values had been righted. She comprehended the true worth of human relationships.

Struggling with her marital relationship, a woman sought an attorney to represent her in a divorce suit. After listing all the reasons why she wanted to end her marriage and all the personal property that she wanted assigned to her, she asked her attorney, "Will I win?" He replied, "Mrs. Simpson, nobody wins in a divorce." Life's real values are in relationships.

One Sunday I shared this message about relationships in a church in California. A couple whom I had counseled on several occasions happened to be present. The wife had separated from her husband, but on the Sunday in question they were enjoying one of their frequent reconciliations. As I explained Naomi's experiences leading up to her new awareness of real values, I prayed earnestly that the Holy Spirit would take the Word of God and apply it to the lives of this couple.

After the service, the couple came up to me as I was greeting worshipers. They both threw their arms around me and hugged me. Then, with tears in their eyes, they said that the story of Naomi and how she had learned the true values in life had done more for them than all the counseling they had received.

I am glad to say that this couple is now happily reconciled. Fortunately, they learned before it was too late that life's true values are to be found in the love and affection shared between a husband and wife and between parents and children.

The Tapestry of Time

How have the women of the village received Ruth? No one pays any attention to her. Not even Naomi mentions her and the sacrifice she has made.

Yet Ruth, within a few weeks, will have won the admiration and respect of the people (cf. 3:11*b*). Furthermore, in time and for Naomi's sake, she will contract a marriage with her late father-in-law's kinsman, Boaz. And later, when her son will be born, these same women who ignore her now, will say to Naomi, "Your daughter-in-law . . . who loves you, is better to you than seven sons" (4:15).

Adverse Winds

So it is that God has a purpose in allowing adversity to come into our lives. He does not forsake us or leave us to our own devices, but as William Cowper wrote, "Behind a frowning providence, He hides a smiling face." In his grace he is able, as Isaiah wrote:

> To comfort all who mourn,
> To give to those who mourn in Zion,
> Giving them a garland [of joy] instead of ashes,
> The oil of gladness instead of mourning,
> The mantle of praise instead of the spirit of fainting
> (61:2*c*–3).

RUTH 1:6–22

PERFECT TIMING

In concluding this section of his story, and as a further evidence of God's grace, the inspired penman both summarized what had happened thus far and also prepared us for what was to follow. He wrote, "And Naomi returned, and with her Ruth the Moabitess, her daughter-in-law, who returned from the fields of Moab; *and they came to Bethlehem at the beginning of the barley harvest*" (1:22, italics added).

Years before when God had given his chosen people the laws that were to govern their lives in the land of Canaan, he had made specific provision for the poor. He built into the legislation of his people a decree that, at harvest time, the poor in the land should glean ears of grain dropped by the reapers during the harvesting process.

In accordance with his nature, and as evidence of his concern for Naomi, he brought Naomi and Ruth back to Bethlehem "at the beginning of the barley harvest (April/May)." They would not go hungry.

THE UNSEEN HAND

God was present in the lives of Naomi and Ruth. He orchestrated everything from Naomi's hearing of the prosperity of her people to the return of both Naomi and Ruth at the very beginning of the harvest.

Many of us have defective views of God. Depending on our outward circumstances, we may view him as a "cosmic policeman" who, at best, will blow the whistle on us if he sees us having any fun but is often ready to arrest us if we do anything wrong. To others he is an "absent landlord" who periodically, and without announcement, invades our lives, checks up on us, and penalizes us for all the errors of omission and commission we have made. In either of these examples, God is looked on as a harsh, unreasonable deity, who is totally unsympathetic with our desires or aspirations, problems or limitations.

Others have a purely utilitarian view of God. They view him as a "cosmic bellboy" who is responsible for answering their every prayer, for running to their aid whenever they get into trouble or have a particular need of him. When not needed, he is to stay out of the way. When those who think of God in purely utilitarian terms find that he does not instantaneously answer their prayers and that some of their desires remain unfulfilled, they begin to doubt his involvement in their lives and wonder if he can be trusted at all. This tends to breed disillusionment and, eventually, the attitude, "Well, I'll just have to get along as best I can, for God cannot be relied on to help me when I need him."

How dramatically these false concepts of God change when we consider his loving-kindness for Naomi, Orpah, and Ruth. This does not mean that he did not deal in grace with Mahlon and Chilion. He did. He gave them ten years in which to return to Bethlehem. When they, as the leaders of the family, continued to flout his wishes, he began to accomplish his plan (see 4:13, 18–22; Matt. 1:5–6, 17) in some other way.

Naomi, of course, was unaware of the far-reaching effects of her decision to return to Judah, and so was Ruth. The realities of life and their personal needs crowded out of their minds the broader scope of God's purpose for them and their descendants, but God demonstrated his loving concern for Naomi by leading her back to the place of blessing. There he would amply reward her. And there too, Ruth, who had come to trust under the shadow of *Yahweh's* wings, would find that he would bless her in seemingly impossible ways.

The grace of God led Naomi to acknowledge her former sin (cf. 1:13*b*, 20*b*, 21*b*). Her confession, accompanied by a cathartic expression of her feelings, had the effect of removing the barriers that had been erected between herself and God. She still felt acutely her loss; but as we shall see in Ruth 2, her former jubilant spirit would soon rise above the winds of adversity that had blown over her soul.

The grace of God also led to Ruth's conversion. Blessing, therefore, was already beginning to attend Naomi's obedience. And on the long road home, Naomi had the benefit of Ruth's companionship as she retraced the steps she and Elimelech had taken a little more than a decade before.

The women of Bethlehem clamored around Naomi on her arrival. They saw alterations in her appearance, but they were unconscious of those changes in themselves. The saddest part of all is that they made no response to her sorrow. As Dr. William Taylor has observed:

> None of them invited her home, or offered her hospitality. She was too poor now to be acknowledged in that way; and after the first expressions of surprise at her appearance, they let her severely alone.[30]

RUTH 1:6–22

But God had not forgotten her, nor would he fail to provide for her temporal needs. His timing of her return was perfect (1:22*b*).

The manifestations of God's grace, so evident in this story, should prove an antidote to pride in times of prosperity and to despondency in seasons of adversity. From his working in the life of Naomi we should learn to gladly trust his sovereign will for us even when all other human inclinations might lead us to a different conclusion.

3 | WHAT TO DO WHEN LIFE TUMBLES IN

Ruth
2:1–7

Howard Ruff, in his book *How to Prosper in the Coming Bad Years,* shares with his readers his experience of life's adversity.

It was late November and Thanksgiving was over. He and his family had been painfully reminded of the loss, only five months earlier, of their youngest son. Now shop windows were reminding people that there were only four weeks until Christmas.

On this particular morning Howard Ruff had been called to his office for a special meeting. The past year had been a difficult one. A strike had virtually paralyzed his business. At last there had been a turn for the better, and the future looked promising. Ruff went to his office confident that he would receive help and advice from the people who managed the national company with which he had a speed-reading franchise.

Instead of the expected assistance, Howard Ruff found his franchise cancelled. His banker froze all his assets, and he found himself on the sidewalk with $11.36 in his pocket. He was declared bankrupt. He had no money, no job, and no unemployment insurance.

Insult was added to injury when the San Francisco Bay area newspapers carried the story of his spectacular business collapse. In addition, the Oakland Symphony Finance Committee asked for his resignation because he was an embarrassment to them.

The Ruff household faced a bleak Christmas, but they decided that "such pain, public humiliation and grief were to be put to some positive purpose, for others, as well as themselves." Armed with this determination they tabulated their assets: a strong religious upbringing that stressed a rugged kind of independence, a sound knowledge of economics, and years of acting and singing experience with expertise in persuasion and communication.

With tenacity of purpose Howard Ruff began to build a meaningful future from the traumatized pieces that remained after he hit bottom. In time he repaid all his debts, even though the insolvency forced on him did not require him to do so. And now, ten years later, he has published books that have become national best sellers. He edits the *Ruff Times* through which he counsels his readers on investments, and he hosts his own television talk show called "Ruffhouse."[1]

AT WIT'S END

Naomi and Ruth knew what it was like to be destitute, perhaps even despised and forsaken. Their welcome in Bethlehem soon faded. Poverty in their culture was regarded as a sign of God's displeasure,[2] and so Elimelech's widow, once proud and of the aristocracy, is now left severely alone, except for the companionship of her daughter-in-law.

Naomi and Ruth return to the cottage in Bethlehem, which in happier times had resounded to the laughter of children at play and where in the cool of the evening Naomi had sat and listened as Elimelech told her about the affairs of the day. What memories must have lingered there still. Certainly *now* she realized that to have a husband and children were evidences of God's favor; to lose them was to empty life of all that made it worth living.

A FRIEND IN NEED

Although Naomi and Ruth may have felt as if they were standing at "Wit's End Corner," the inspired writer has provided us with a link in the narrative that prepares us for what was to follow. He did this so subtly that we tend to pass over Ruth 2:1 without paying much attention to what was being said. We need to remember that while Boaz was being introduced to us, Naomi and Ruth were unaware of the part he would play in their future.

Our storyteller wrote:

Now Naomi [had] a relative[3] of her husband, a mighty man of valor, of[4] the [extended] family of Elimelech, and his name was Boaz (2:1).

RUTH 2:1–7

The exact nature of Boaz's relationship to Elimelech was not stated. Some Jewish writers believed Boaz was Elimelech's nephew.[5] The important point for us to notice is that Boaz was related to Elimelech, not Naomi. Had he been related to Naomi, he would not have been able later on to perform the duty of a kinsman.

Boaz was described as an *'îš gibbôr ḥayil*, "a mighty man of valor."[6] Some translators have rendered this expression as if it referred to his wealth. But the usage of this word in the Book of Judges (11:1) as well as in Ruth 3:11 seems to indicate that "valor" is the preferable rendering.[7] These were troubled times, and any man might have to fight to protect his crops or herds, house or land, from the plundering raids of Bedouin or the encroachments of the local Canaanites. Their only law was "might is right" and "I'm entitled to take from you whatever I can."

For the present, all we need to know is that Boaz was destined to become the means whereby the grace of God was extended to Naomi.

WOMAN OF VALOR

As soon as Naomi and Ruth make the cottage livable, Ruth takes on herself the material support of her mother-in-law.

> And Ruth the Moabitess[8] said to Naomi, "Let [me] now go to the field,[9] and glean among the ears of grain after him in whose eyes I shall find favor."[10] And Naomi said to her, "Go, my daughter." So Ruth went, and came [to the field], and gleaned in the field after the reapers; and she happened by chance[11] on the portion of the field [belonging to] Boaz, who [was] of the family of Elimelech (2:2–3).

Although Ruth has only been in Bethlehem a short time, she has already looked about the area to see what she can do to support her mother-in-law. She is proactive, not reactive. She does not wait for something to happen but takes the initiative. In this she sets a good example for those in a similar situation.

Different people respond to adversity and the painful reverses of life in different ways. Some become passive and expect everything to be done for them. As their dependency on others increases, they also tend to cling to them for support.

Others, according to Dr. William Hulme in his book, *Creative Loneliness,* become self-centered. They indulge themselves.[12] Either

RUTH 2:1–7

for the sake of security or out of a desire to believe that someone wants them, they may engage in promiscuous sexual relationships (in contrast to Ruth in 3:10*b*).

Relatively few are able to make with ease the adjustments of culture and status that Ruth made and also undertake the support of another person.

All of this was not lost on the author of the book. That was why at the beginning of chapter 2, he reminded us that Ruth was a foreigner. She was a stranger in a strange land.

"But what," we may ask, "is required of a person if he or she is to surmount the adversities that invariably come one's way?"

Modern research has identified five characteristics that are of fundamental importance to each one of us if we are to triumph over the vicissitudes of our human existence and lead happy, effective, fulfilled lives. They are:

- our sense of personal autonomy
- our sexuality (i.e., how we think of ourselves as men or women)
- our internalized sense of morality
- our career choice
- our hope for the future.[13]

We will consider each of these and seek to ascertain from the biblical record how they apply to the heroine of our story.

A Time for Boldness

Without waiting for any prompting, Ruth tells Naomi, "Let me now go to the field and glean." She is appropriately assertive and at the same time willingly subordinate to her mother-in-law. She is a stranger and naturally looks to Naomi for guidance in matters of local custom. But this has not made her passive. Her ability to see needs and try to meet them indicates her freedom of thought and decisiveness.

In seeking a place to begin gleaning, Ruth goes down to the field where the reapers are. She is unaware of the fact that God, in his grace, is leading her to "the portion of the field belonging to Boaz." Her plan is to find someone in whose eyes she will find favor. On seeing a foreman supervising the reapers, she asks for permission to gather up the grain that had fallen to the ground.[14]

The manner in which Ruth speaks to the young man placed over the reapers shows that she does not presume on his favor or on her rights as an alien. The Law specifically stated that the poor and strangers were to be allowed to glean in the fields at harvest time (Lev. 19:9ff., 23:22; Deut. 24:19). Ruth, however, is not obtrusive. Instead, she requests to be allowed to glean between the sheaves. If denied permission, she apparently was prepared to persevere with her quest until some other foreman gave his consent (2:2). Such resilience was an outgrowth of a well-balanced personality and showed a well-developed sense of autonomy.

In most cultures an individual's sense of autonomy is developed prior to one's leaving home. Skills are cultivated that prepare a person to function and be self-supporting. Generally speaking, physical maturation is important to proper autonomy, for certain functions require a measure of strength, coordination, and endurance.

In addition, the process of identification and the accompanying internalization of values (which will be discussed below) assist an individual in adopting an appropriate and comfortable style of behavior. One aspect of this behavior is seen in independence of action.

Autonomy also necessitates the development of mental and emotional maturity. On the one hand, as a person grows, he acquires a certain amount of knowledge. This is evident in job preference (based on one's experience of success), problem-solving ability, and planning for the future. Emotional maturity is also needed. This often takes the form of being able to establish lasting relationships outside the home, possessing the capacity for intimacy, and letting go of the last apron strings of dependency on parents.

As we compare these broad principles of personal autonomy to Ruth's experience, we find that she, of her own volition, left her father and mother and the country of her birth for a land that previously was unknown to her (2:11). Such an act required considerable personal maturity.

As a newcomer to Bethlehem, Ruth faced a problem. How would she support Naomi? Ruth solved this problem by doing what she could as first one opportunity and then another presented themselves. Her long-range planning was perhaps best seen in chapter 3 where she asks Boaz to marry her so that Naomi will be cared for. Her actions throughout these chapters reflected her emotional maturity, for she was always thinking of others, not herself.

Further investigation reveals that autonomy is intimately connected with the way people view themselves as individuals. In a

word, a person's *sexuality*—i.e., how a man thinks of himself as a
man and how a woman thinks of herself as a woman.

The Issue of Sexuality

Mature sex-role identity may be traced back to a child's relationship with his or her parents, and particularly the one of the same
sex. From their fathers, boys learn what is required of men, the
social expectations or standards set for them, and how they are to
relate to women. From their mothers, girls learn what women are
like, how to perform the duties that fall within the domain of a wife
and mother, who may also work outside the home, and how they
should relate to men.

Later on both boys and girls develop heterosexual relationships
and experience the pressure from their parents for mature sex-role
behavior. During this stage in their development, young men are
expected to give promise of being able to hold a steady job and
provide for a family, and young women are expected to develop
discrete patterns of behavior and acquire those maternal skills that
help them become good wives and mothers.

In the case of Ruth, we have good reason to believe that her ten-
year marriage to Mahlon was a happy one. Although children were
denied her, she gives every evidence of being the kind of wife who
was loving and affectionate toward her husband, as well as appropriately supportive of him. As a widow and an alien, Ruth was in an
invidious position. The work that she had chosen as a means of
supporting herself and Naomi was not without its hazards. As Dr.
Samuel Cox has pointed out, the "reapers were apt to be vicious and
rude," especially to strangers (2:9*a*). "All through this chapter we
see that Ruth ran a great risk [of sexual abuse]"[15] (see also 2:22).

Two types of people are most liable to sexual harassment. They
are those who flaunt their sexuality and those who are shy and
retiring. One who is comfortable in her role as a woman can steer a
middle course, be noticed, and yet escape molestation. In Ruth's
case, we notice that the young man who was placed over the reapers
was sufficiently attracted to her to watch her (2:7).

From all that is revealed to us, we gather that Ruth was winsome
and possessed a feminine mystique that made her attractive to others. Yet she did not flaunt her sexuality or use it to gain the ends she
sought. She appeared confident in her role as a woman and free

from any need to draw attention to herself. Further evidence of her attractiveness as a woman came from Boaz himself (3:10*b*). He said that she could have her pick of any of the young men of the village. They were obviously attracted to her, but she did not encourage them.

Ruth's situation held a built-in danger. To use the biblical terminology (2:5*b*), she did not "belong" to any man,[16] and so she had no one to protect her. And being a foreigner from a despised race, she was even more vulnerable. This was why Boaz instructed his servants not to abuse (or insult) her.

People's sense of autonomy and how they view themselves as either a man or a woman forms an integral part of the way they think about themselves. Their internalized morality further contributes to this self-understanding.

A Question of Right and Wrong

According to those students of human nature who have thoroughly researched modern man's moral development, there are three levels or stages in one's progress toward a mature sense of right and wrong.[17] These stages of development are: (1) a concern with the external consequences of one's acts and the power of those who are authority figures in our lives; (2) the maintaining of an existing rule structure with due respect for authority; and (3) a commitment of oneself to a personal or universal set of moral principles.

The process of growth may be seen as a search for a set of values that will preserve integrity and guide behavior. The decisions that people make are therefore an evidence of the moral principles to which they have committed themselves.

How Ruth's Moabite ancestry affected her moral development is uncertain, but she had a surprisingly well-defined internalized set of standards that freed her from the fear of disapproval. Her conduct was not controlled by rituals, peer groups, or externalized standards of morality. All her actions give us the feeling that she was acting in complete freedom. She appeared to have a mature value system that guided her behavior and, in spite of pressures brought to bear on her, enabled her to handle the reverses of life without violating her integrity.

Ruth had been able to shun the many licentious practices of her people and also avoid the legalism that frequently characterized the zealous Hebrew. She seemed to enjoy a life of freedom from both of these extremes. As a result, she was happy in herself, joyful in her new-found faith, and ready to give of herself for the sake of her mother-in-law. No wonder people found her attractive.

Love's Labor

In addition to a sense of personal autonomy, a clearly-defined sense of sexuality, and an internalized sense of morality, a person's choice of a career is an important part of one's identity. It sets the stage for one's adult life-style. It determines one's daily routine, associates, and social status. It is also a direct or indirect reflection of one's system of values.

Normally, when counseling young people regarding their choice of a career, I recommend that they keep their options open; evaluate possible professions in light of their personal investigation, introspection, and self-evaluation; and weigh possible openings in light of their skills, temperament, values, and future goals.

When older people face job loss, the first thing they do is consider their options. What possibilities are open to them? These may be fewer than when they were younger.

As we consider the situation in which Ruth found herself, we realize that she was not permitted the luxury of too many options. Job opportunities for her were virtually nonexistent. Being a charwoman or, if she was still young and attractive, a "prostitute," were about the only two "vocations" that widows in Old Testament times could follow.[18] In Ruth's case, we find her willing to take whatever menial work she could find. In her culture, there were no other alternatives, except seasonal ones like harvesting.

God in his grace had brought Naomi and Ruth back to Bethlehem at the beginning of the barley harvest. Seeing the reapers going out to the field, Ruth determined to join them. "Nor was she scrupulous as to the sort of industry in which she might engage," wrote Dr. William Taylor:

> It might be true that she had been in comfortable circumstances, and had never needed to do any kind of outdoor work while her husband lived; but she accepted the situation now, and was willing to do anything, however lowly, if only it were honest, for her own and her mother's livelihood. She did not dictate to Providence, or say that if she could get this or that she would take it, but she could

never bring herself to do that other. Rather she is willing to take any honorable course that might open to her, and, as gleaning was the first that presented itself, she would take that, unless Naomi objected.

It is always hard for those who have been in comfort and are reduced to destitution to bring this willinghood to take what offers, and perhaps it was easier for Ruth to act on such a determination in Bethlehem than it would have been in Moab, among those who had known her when she was better off. But in all cases, *that* is the surest way out of penury, and the sooner it is taken the shorter is the road.[19]

Ray of Hope

All of this brings us to consider the one ingredient that is indispensable to life, namely, *hope*. People need and, in fact, must have hope. Without it there is only increasing discouragement and eventual despair.

Boaz verbalizes Ruth's hope when he says, *"Yahweh* shall repay your work, and your reward shall be complete from *Yahweh,* the God of Israel, under whose wings you have come to take refuge" (2:12).

The apostle Paul too had hope in the midst of adversity. On the basis of his confidence in God's ability to undertake for his own, he could write those in Corinth, "We are being afflicted in every [way], but not crushed; in difficulties but not despairing; persecuted, but not deserted; struck down, but not destroyed; . . . we do not lose heart . . . for our momentary, light affliction is producing for us an eternal weight of glory. . . ." (2 Cor. 4:8–9, 16–17). And each of us must have some form of hope, too, or else we are left with nothing to look forward to but a bleak future.

Ruth's new faith in the one true God gave her hope as she faced the uncertainties of life. As she rose to meet the challenge before her, she drew on inner resources; and as we shall see, in a few short weeks, she impressed everyone in Bethlehem with her winsomeness and character (3:11*b*).

As it was with Ruth, so it is with us. Our sense of personal autonomy, the way we think of ourselves, our internalized sense of morality, our career choice, and our confidence in the Lord help us face life and overcome the tensions and setbacks that are a part of everyone's experience.

RUTH 2:1–7

FIRST IMPRESSIONS

At this juncture the biblical writer made an abrupt change in what he had been recording. He drew our attention away from Ruth to Boaz. He wrote:

> And behold,[20] Boaz came from Bethlehem and said to the reapers, *"Yahweh* be with you."[21] And they replied, "May *Yahweh* bless you." And Boaz said to his young man[22] set over his reapers, "Whose [is] this young woman?"[23] And the young man set over the reapers answered and said, "A young Moabitess woman[24] who returned with Naomi from the fields of Moab. And she asked, 'Please let me glean, and I will gather among the sheaves,[25] after the reapers'; and she came and has remained from [early] morning[26] until now; [except that] she sat a little while in the house" (2:4–7).

In these verses, we are given

> a graphic picture of an ancient harvest scene. The field is thick with waving barley. The reapers cut their way into it with sickles, grasping the ears till their arms are full. Behind them the women gather up the armfuls and bind them into sheaves. Still farther in the rear follow the widow and stranger, who, according to the Hebrew law, have the right to glean after the reapers. The overseer is busily urging on the reapers and granting or refusing admission to the gleaners. [Skins filled with water hang from the branch of a nearby tree, kept cool by the soft breeze. A "house" is also there in which those who are weary may rest from the glare and heat of the sun.] Here, too, under the shade of some spreading tree, men and women gather at mealtime, and are supplied with parched corn . . . which they dip in a cool and strengthening mixture of vinegar and oil and water.[27]

Onto this scene Boaz comes. Our first impression of him is most favorable. He is gracious and cordial, showing through his greeting of the reapers that he is a man of keen spiritual sensitivity. He also appears to be conscious of the fact that all blessing comes from the Lord, and he desires God's blessing to be experienced by the reapers as well. He therefore greets them in the name of the Lord.

Boaz takes a kindly interest in Bethlehem's poor who are gleaning in his field. Theirs is backbreaking work, and a day of hard labor would meet an entire family's needs for only a few days.

The writer tacitly intimated that Boaz knows personally all of those in his field, for when he sees one whom he does not know, he inquires about her. The stranger he has noticed, of course, is Ruth. The question Boaz puts to his overseer is revealing: "To whom does this young woman belong?" (2:5*b*). He presumes that she is married and has recently come to live in the village with her husband.

Boaz receives an interesting response. The article is missing from the young man's reply as if he is implying that Ruth, being poor and not of Israel, is hardly worth noticing. We might perhaps paraphrase the young man's reply to Boaz as follows: "She's a young Moabitess; [the] one who came back with Naomi." She is too insignificant to be identified by name.

In that single sentence the overseer shows us a great deal about himself. He is conscious of social rank and national pride and where everyone stands (or should stand) in the pecking order. He is obviously informed and for that reason his words are valuable to Boaz, but by his actions Boaz shows us that he does not accept his assistant's system of values (2:8ff).

But something else is of importance in the young man's response to Boaz's inquiry. Although he probably would have denied that Ruth was anything but a foreigner, she had made an impression on him, and he had been watching her. He even noticed when she went and took a brief rest under the shelter[28] that had been built for the benefit of the workers.

With little statements like these, he betrayed the mixed emotions within him; and we, by our words, tend to do the same.

EASILY OVERLOOKED FACTS

The young overseer's description of the way in which Ruth approached him, as well as her conduct in the field, enlarges our understanding as well as our appreciation of her. Her "please let me glean" was phrased delicately and anticipated an affirmative answer. She was gracious and positive in her attitude. She had suffered much, but she was not depressed (cf. 2:11*b*). The setbacks of the past few weeks had not left her in despair. She may have been beaten down by the sheer weight of her trials, but she still had confidence in herself and in the one under whose wings she had taken refuge (cf. 2:12*b*). And on account of her love for her mother-in-law, she was determined to persevere.

Under such circumstances insecurity, apprehension over the future, and concern for the next meal might lead to frantic activity.

Was this true of Ruth? Boaz's servant describes her activity (2:7*b*). She started early, worked diligently; and when she was tired, she rested. Evidently Ruth was sufficiently secure in herself and confident in the Lord not to allow her anxieties to goad her into unwarranted activity. No evidence in the story suggested that fear of impoverishment drove her to the border of panic. She worked hard, and when she felt the need, she relaxed.

All of this points to Ruth's well-rounded personality. It also provides a good model for our own efforts. We may not be in the same straights, but our work should be as diligent. We do not need to use our work as an outlet for our neuroses (i.e., become workaholics). Ruth did not, in spite of a situation that might have made such conduct excusable.

In company with Ruth, Howard Ruff, and many, many others, we all, at one time or another, experience the trials and setbacks of life. How we overcome the vicissitudes of life is dependent on two things: (1) the way we think of ourselves;[29] and (2) our confidence in the Lord. Ruth illustrates for us the personal dynamics that will help us rise up from the ashes of our experience and persevere. She also shows us how God graciously works behind the scenes to accomplish his purpose for us. Although we may not be aware of his involvement, his guidance of us is as sure as his direction of Ruth's footsteps to the portion of the field that belonged to Boaz. We may therefore trust him to work *in us* as well as in our circumstances. In time he will lead our footsteps to a brighter pathway.

THE DYNAMICS OF THE HELPING RELATIONSHIP

4

Ruth
2:8–17

Dr. Charles R. Swindoll, internationally known for his ability to expound the Scriptures with insight and understanding, told in one of his messages about a television program on the Library of Congress.

The program had all the markings of a slow-moving, dull documentary.

About halfway through, Dr. Daniel Boorstin, our librarian of Congress, brought out a little box from a small closet that once held the library's rarities. The label on the box read: CONTENTS OF THE PRESIDENT'S POCKETS ON THE NIGHT OF APRIL 14, 1865.

Since that was the fateful night Abraham Lincoln was assassinated, every viewer's attention was seized.

Boorstin then proceeded to remove the items in the small container and display them on camera. There were five things in the box:

- handkerchief embroidered "A. Lincoln"
- a country boy's pen knife
- a spectacles case repaired with string
- a purse containing a $5 bill—*Confederate money (!)*
- some old and worn newspaper clippings.

"The clippings," said Boorstin, "were concerned with the great deeds of Abraham Lincoln. And one of them actually reports a speech by John Bright which says that Abraham Lincoln is one of the greatest men of all times."

Today, that's common knowledge. The world now knows that British statesman John Bright was right in his assessment of Lincoln, but in 1865 millions shared quite a contrary opinion. The President's critics were fierce and many. His was a lonely agony that reflected the suffering and turmoil of a country ripped to shreds by hatred and a cruel, costly war.

There is something touchingly pathetic in the mental picture of this great leader seeking solace and self-assurance from the comfort of a few old newspaper clippings as he reads them under the flickering flame of a candle all alone in the Oval office."[1]

All of this brings us to consider the importance of encouragement and the way in which we can best use a unique gift of the Spirit that we all share—*the gift of helps.*

BIBLICAL EXAMPLES

Two people in Scripture clearly illustrated the gift of helps: Boaz and Barnabas.

Barnabas's real name was Joseph.[2] He was given the nickname *bar Nabas,* "son of consolation" or "son of encouragement" (Acts 4:36), because he was always helping people. He ministered to believers in the church in Jerusalem during times of persecution. As with his Master before him, he went about doing good. He helped the afflicted, comforted the distressed, and encouraged the downhearted. He even braved the censure of those in Jerusalem by introducing the recently converted persecutor of Christians, Paul, to the leaders of the church.

The other prominent biblical personality who illustrated the gift of helps was Boaz. His name, in all probability, meant "in him is strength." He was a kinsman of Naomi's late husband, Elimelech (2:1), but apparently the relationship was not close enough for him to be linked with Bethlehem's aristocracy.[3] He was referred to as an *'îš gibbôr ḥayil,* "a mighty man of valor." He was undoubtedly brave and resourceful—the kind of person the people of Bethlehem were glad to have as the leader of their little militia. Such a man was needed to protect their crops and herds from the Bedouin or Canaanites who would plunder and carry off their few possessions.

When Boaz came down from the city to the harvest field, he greeted his reapers sincerely. He was not so preoccupied that he overlooked the poor who had come to glean in his field. As Dr. Robert Watson has observed, "From the moment he appears in the narrative we note in him a certain largeness of character."[4] And he was right. In Boaz, piety, kindness, generosity, and empathy were finely blended. It is no wonder that from the events of this chapter we learn the *how* as well as the *what* of the helping relationship.

PAST, PRESENT, AND PERSONAL

As we take up the story, we see Boaz's kindly interest in a stranger who is gleaning in his field.

> And Boaz said to Ruth, "Do you not hear, my daughter?[5] Do not go to glean in another field, and also[6] do not leave this [one]; and you shall stay[7] with my young women. Your eyes[8] [shall be] on the field which they shall reap,[9] and you shall go after them;[10] have I not ordered the young men not to touch you?[11] When you [are] thirsty, then you shall go to the vessels and shall drink[12] from that which the young men draw" (2:8–9).

Boaz apparently is impressed with the report of his young overseer. He observes how diligently Ruth picks up the ears of grain that have fallen to the ground. He is filled with admiration for her, knowing that she is working hard in order to be able to support Naomi. He calls her to him and, in words of positive assurance, impresses on her the fact that she is welcome to glean in his field. In fact, he goes a step further and, with kindly insistence, says that she is not to go to any other field. Then, realizing that Ruth is not able to distinguish one field from another, he encourages her to keep close to his maids.

Up to this point, nothing has been done by anyone in Bethlehem to make Ruth feel accepted. It is probable that, as a foreigner, she has been subjected to proud and scornful looks and a we'll-wait-and-see-how-she-turns-out kind of attitude. In time, Ruth will win the hearts of everyone in the village (cf. 3:11*b*, 4:11–12), but up until now she has had to struggle along on her own.

But why was Boaz so kind to Ruth?

Robert Watson remarked, "The truth was that Ruth had met with a man of character who valued character."

Notice too the wisdom of his actions. He was kind without being patronizing. He made her feel accepted: "You shall stay with my young women."

Then, he was also considerate of her well-being: "I have ordered the young men not to touch you."

RUTH 2:8–17

Finally, he facilitated the work she was doing by maximizing her time: "When you are thirsty [instead of going all the way back to Bethlehem] drink from the water my young men have drawn."

In these few verses, we have important keys to the helping relationship.

Accentuating the Positive

In the first place, Boaz was kind without being condescending. Without causing Ruth to feel any loss of respect for herself, or without producing any undue dependence on him, Boaz assured Ruth of his willingness to help her. In doing so, he did not deprive her of the dignity of honest toil. He did assure her of her acceptance in his field.

Often in our desire to help others we try to do everything for them. We make them feel dependent on us. When this happens, we erode their sense of esteem—that God-given right to derive satisfaction from their honest labor. Then they begin to feel inferior. Resentment begins to develop, and with resentment comes a latent hostility. Then, later on, we are surprised when those whom we have helped the most turn on us and castigate us. To use the old cliché, they "bite the hand that fed them." Why? We did the right thing in the wrong way.

Boaz could easily have been patronizing. He wasn't because he was wise enough to be helpful without robbing Ruth of the right to work.

Feeling of Isolation

Second, Boaz removed any feeling of isolation by encouraging Ruth to stay close to his young women. This gave her a sense of acceptance, of belonging.

People who are in need of help desire this same feeling of acceptance and belonging. Their lives have been disrupted. Others seem not to care or to be preoccupied with their own concerns. What they need to experience is a genuine feeling of "I believe in you," "I approve of you," "I'm not afraid to be identified with you."

Boaz made Ruth feel wanted.

RUTH 2:8–17

Basic Issues

Third, Boaz was considerate of Ruth's well-being. He was aware of certain habit patterns and knew how easily the men in his employ might take advantage of a foreigner. He took precautions to insure Ruth's safety.

Those who have watched the movie *Billy Jack* know how easily boisterous "fun" can lead to an untimely death. Our helpfulness of others should not expose them to abuse. Instead, we should be sensitive to the possibility of their being hurt and, wherever possible, take steps to prevent it.

Boaz knew how easy it would be for Ruth—poor and from Moab—to be looked on as having no rights in Judah, so he instructed the young men not to harass or molest her.

Boaz was considerate of Ruth's well-being while on the job. He knew from experience how thirsty a person became when he or she worked in the open field under the heat of the summer sun. To have to walk all the way to Bethlehem, draw water to quench one's thirst, and then return to the field, would waste a considerable amount of time. To facilitate Ruth's gathering of the grain, Boaz helped her maximize her time by giving her permission to drink from the water drawn by the young men.

The importance of helping others cannot be overstressed. Helpers give friendly guidance and timely precautions and anticipate people's needs. This is very confirming. The importance of these acts in the helping relationship cannot be overstressed. Our friendly guidance, timely warnings, and thoughtful considerations can make a person feel accepted, valued, and competent. Without a helping spirit, our best efforts on behalf of others will tarnish before our eyes. With it, we will encourage others.

FADING STIGMA

Ruth responds in gratitude to Boaz's kindly, considerate attitude. She is overwhelmed and quickly sinks to her knees; then she touches her forehead to the ground before him. The text reads:

And she fell on her face, and bowed herself[13] to the earth, and said to him, "Why have I found favor in your eyes, that you should notice me, and I a stranger?"[14] And Boaz said to her, "All that you have done for [lit., with] your mother-in-law after the death of your husband,

RUTH 2:8–17

has been fully[15] told me; and how you forsook your father, and your mother, and the land of your birth, and came to a people whom you had not known before.[16] May *Yahweh* repay your work,[17] and may your wages [be] complete from *Yahweh,* the God of Israel, under whose wings[18] you have come to take refuge." And Ruth said, "May I continue to find favor in your eyes,[19] my lord, because you have spoken to the heart of [i.e., have cheered] your handmaid, though I am not as one of your handmaids"[20] (2:10–13).

Ruth is deeply touched by Boaz's magnanimity. She has not presumed on his kindness. Her intentions that morning were to glean enough grain for herself and Naomi. Now, she has been shown remarkable benevolence by a man she has only just met. She knows nothing of Boaz's relationship to her late father-in-law, but she is curious and inquires why he has shown her favor.

Boaz explains that he has fully been told all that she has done for Naomi since Mahlon died. He is aware that, as with Abraham before her, she has left her home and family and country for an unknown land. He prays that *Yahweh* will recompense her fully. Here is the encouragement she needs. Here too is the promise of hope for the future. As Dr. Leon Morris has said, "[These words] represent the first cheerful thing recorded as happening to her since the death of her husband."[21] How easy they were to utter . . . and how necessary.

Ruth's response is one of grateful recognition. She is not one of Boaz's handmaidens (*šiphāt*) and places herself below even those of Boaz's household who do the most menial work. In this we see her true humility.

In the words that pass between Boaz and Ruth we observe the kindness of Boaz matched by the graciousness of Ruth. He was prosperous, but he did not allow his good fortune to cause him to forget the poor. She had been reduced to poverty, but had not permitted such a reversal of fortune to make her hard and cynical.

In this respect, Dr. G. Campbell Morgan was right when he pointed out that the lives of Boaz and Ruth illustrated saintship. In spite of difficulties too numerous to mention, Ruth flourished amid circumstances calculated to discourage her. Boaz lived amid people of privilege in times of degeneracy, yet without permitting the social mores of his day to squeeze him into their mold.

Both Ruth and Boaz displayed a unique trust in the Lord. They prove: (1) that outward circumstances neither make nor mar the children of God; (2) that faith still is the key to appropriating the blessings of God; and (3) that through obedience to the revealed will of God, he makes us part of a plan that exceeds our ability to imagine.[22]

RURAL HOSPITALITY

Boaz has already made Ruth feel accepted, valued, and able. In a word, he has encouraged her. Now he introduces her to the circle of his workers. He desires that they receive her with typical rural hospitality.

And Boaz said to Ruth at mealtime,[23] "Come here, and you shall eat of the bread and dip your morsel in the vinegar."[24] And she sat at the side of the harvesters. And Boaz served[25] her roasted grain,[26] and she ate and was satisfied and had some left over.[27] When she arose to glean, Boaz commanded his young men, saying, "She may glean[28] even among the sheaves, and [do not do anything that would] shame her.[29] And also you shall purposely pull out for her [some grain] from the bundles and shall leave it; and she shall glean and you shall not rebuke her." So Ruth gleaned in the field until evening. Then she beat out what she had gleaned, and it was about an ephah of barley (2:14–17).

The scene these verses describe has been observed by travelers in the Middle East. Dr. Edward Robinson told of what he saw while on a visit to the Holy Land.

In one field, as we approached Kubeibeh, nearly 200 reapers and gleaners were at work; the latter being nearly as numerous as the former. A few were taking their refreshment, and offered us some of their "parched corn." In the season of harvest the grains of wheat, not yet fully dry and hard, are roasted in a pan or on an iron plate, and constitute a very palatable article of food. This is eaten with bread, or instead of it. Indeed, the use of it is so common at this time among the laboring classes, that this parched wheat is sold in markets. . . . The whole scene of the reapers and gleaners, and their "parched corn," gave us a lively representation of the story of Ruth and ancient harvest-time in the fields of Boaz.[30]

Boaz eats *with* his servants. He does not feel the need to keep them at a distance. Men of character do not need to enforce respect. They have earned it because of *what* (not who) they are. They need no artificial hierarchy, titles, or tokens of superiority. They are as-

RUTH 2:8–17

sured and confident, so they do not require the homage of those of lower social status.

Ruth has a sense of assurance. She has only recently told Boaz that she is not even to be numbered among his *šiphāt,* or "maidservants," a more menial designation even than *'amâh,* "handmaid." Yet when invited to join him for the noonday meal, she is able to do so without any false modesty or embarrassment.

Boaz performs the duty of a host by serving Ruth himself. In this we see his special kindness. Such action would be noticed by his servants, and out of respect for so kind an employer, they would be more inclined to treat Ruth the same way.

The additional food Ruth receives also indicates Boaz's special favor. It recalls to mind Joseph, as prime minister of Egypt, entertaining his brothers and giving Benjamin five times as much as any of the others (cf. Gen. 43:34).

Furthermore, Boaz instructs his servants to allow Ruth to glean in between the standing sheaves and also tells them to purposely drop small bundles for her to pick up as she works along behind them. He is concerned that Ruth's efforts on behalf of Naomi be amply rewarded.

Boaz's servants cooperate so well that by evening Ruth has to beat out what she has gathered before she can take it home. Although it is difficult to know exactly how much an ephah was, authorities claim that its weight was about thirty pounds.

A HELPING HAND

All of this brings us to consider the essence of the helping relationship—*encouragement,* the kind of encouragement that meets a person's physiological and psychological needs. Ruth's physiological needs were basic: food, shelter, and clothing. In our story, hunger was a very real threat to both her and her mother-in-law. Ruth's psychological needs were likewise basic. She needed to feel accepted, valued, and capable.

Bruised Expectations

One of our most basic needs is for a sense of acceptance or belongingness. When all is going well, we tend to take the blessings of life for granted. We are content if we can keep our trials under

RUTH 2:8–17

control. When adversity strikes, our friends frequently desert us. They have enough problems of their own without taking on any of ours (unlike Gal. 6:2). At a time like this we are tempted to feel we do not belong, that nobody cares, and that we are all alone.

The exercise of the gift of helps begins with an acceptance of the person. This is a rare quality today, for all of us feel depersonalized. To the IRS we are a computer number; to the state or federal government we are a statistic; and to charitable organizations we represent a potential contribution. We all need to feel wanted, to be accepted, to be a part of a community; and never is this more true than when we are hurting. Those who desire to be used of God to lift up the downcast and heal broken hearts must, therefore, begin with the acceptance of the individual. Such an attitude encourages those who are experiencing the unjust inequities or capricious reverses of life.

Uncertain Future

Helpers accept others, but they also uplift another's personal worth. Anxieties over one's safety or questions about whether life holds any promise of anything better may reduce a person's effectiveness. This, in turn, may hinder individuals from getting back on their feet.

Boaz knew the risks associated with the harvesting of crops and took immediate steps to ensure Ruth's personal safety. To him she was a person of worth, not the member of a despised race. This done, Ruth could put forth her best effort.

This sense of being valued by another, of being of worth (or significance) for who you are rather than for the work you do, is something sorely needed in commerce and industry, education and politics, church and society. Without it we feel depersonalized; with it we feel accepted and assured. All too often in our homes as well as our businesses people are treated like things, and things are invested with worth as if they were people. Such a breakdown in the interpersonal process leads to the establishment of adversary relationships in which workers do as little for their employers as possible. Then employers feel they must exert pressure on their employees in order to get them to work at even marginal levels of efficiency.

RUTH 2:8–17

How beautifully Boaz illustrated for us the difference respect for the person makes in one's attitude. And through his conduct, others imbibed his outlook.

Timely Assistance

Recognizing the importance of acceptance and personal worth, helpers take a third step—they assist others, maximizing the needy's own efforts.

I recall my mother describing some timely help given her by her pastor's wife. My mother and brother were moving into a new home. The previous owners had a maid. She had cooked for her employers and kept house for them. The house was immaculate; the kitchen was a mess.

On the day my mother moved in she found, so she said, "Ten years of dust, pieces of stale bread, hardened spaghetti, and old pop bottle tops against the wall where the refrigerator had stood." (Her pastor's wife concurred, saying this was the filthiest kitchen she had ever seen.) The stove and oven represented an accumulation of grime and grease that had not been removed since their installation.

All the joy of moving into a new house was gone. Cleaning the kitchen had taken on Himalayan proportions. Just then the doorbell rang. The movers had arrived with all the furniture and at least 132 boxes of assorted shapes and sizes.

To the credit of the pastor's wife, she tackled the kitchen, sweeping away a decade of accumulated dust and garbage, cleaning unbelievable grime from the stove and oven, and scrubbing the floor. This one room alone took an entire day to clean.

The result? My mother could maximize her time and energies, showing the movers where the furniture should go and then unpacking and putting into closets the contents of the boxes. Only my mother really knows how encouraging it was to have such timely help.

NO LONGER HOPELESS

The ministry of helping others is essentially a ministry of encouragement. Ruth acknowledged this. She said to Boaz, "You have spoken to the heart of your maidservant" (2:13). His words and attitudes heartened her.

RUTH 2:8–17

The steps that Boaz took are the same for all who wish to use the gift of helps. They included:

- Accepting individuals as they are and making them feel that they belong
- Treating them as people of worth and insuring that their rights are respected
- Assisting them in obtaining the best results from their time and resources.

Such a ministry of encouragement is open to everyone of us. Jonathan engaged in it when he sought out David at Horesh and "strengthened his hands in God" (1 Sam. 23:15–18). He emboldened his friend to look away from himself to the one who is a very present Helper of those who are in trouble (Ps. 46:1).

The apostle Paul exhorted the believers to constantly be encouraging one another and building one another up in the faith (1 Thess. 5:11). Isaiah spoke about encouraging those who are exhausted with life's conflicts and strengthening those who feel that they cannot go on any more (Isa. 35:3). And Paul, who knew how much we all need a lifting up of our spirits, spoke of the encouragement that comes to our hearts as we meditate on God's Word (Rom. 15:4).

Such encouragement will enable those who are cast down to enjoy a measure of happiness and contentment, regardless of their temporal circumstances.

RUTH 2:8–17

⫷ GOD'S PROVISION
5⎤ FOR MAN'S NEED

Ruth
2:18–23

Certain words need no explanation: *Rolls Royce. NASA. Patriotism. Touchdown.* They are synonymous with quality of workmanship, space exploration, pride in one's country, and the discipline and teamwork that always precedes achievement.

In his book, *Six Great Ideas,* Mortimer Adler discussed certain other words: *truth, goodness, beauty* (the standards by which we assess worth), and *liberty, equality, justice* (the principles that govern our actions). Dr. Adler said, "The words that name the great ideas are all of them words of ordinary, everyday speech. They do not belong to the private jargon of a specialized branch of knowledge."[1] However, the very fact that Mortimer Adler has found it necessary to write an entire book about them indicates how little we understand their real meaning.

Other words must likewise be explained, for our perceptions about them are hazy and ill-defined. These words include: *character, wealth, happiness,* and *devotion.*

We found in chapter 4 that the two great tests of character were wealth and poverty. In the case of Boaz, we learned that a true test of character may be found in the way in which a person treats those who can do nothing for him. In the next chapter, we will observe that another test of character is what a person does in the dark, not in the light when actions are in plain view.

We too often equate having money with being happy. We have been reared to believe that the Constitution guarantees us the right to "life, liberty, and the *purchase* of happiness." Few realize that riches do not bring happiness.

Howard Hughes died in April 1976. He had amassed a fortune estimated at two billion dollars. Shortly before becoming a recluse, the industrialist, aviator, and filmmaker was interviewed by a reporter. The conversation was taped and played by "NBC News" the night Hughes died. One of the questions asked the billionaire was whether or not his wealth and power had brought him any lasting happiness.

"No," replied Hughes, "I would not say that I am a happy man!"[2]

Happiness is not in abundant possessions or avid pursuits, but in an inner contentment and in enjoying what we have to do. True happiness is more a matter of personality than surroundings. It is found in the contentment that fills the soul even in the midst of the most distressing circumstances. That is why one sage remarked, "If you can't find contentment in yourself, it is useless to seek for it elsewhere."

And then there is devotion—the dedication of one's entire being to a person or a cause. In the case of Ruth, her devotion was to her mother-in-law. She did not regard the care of Naomi as a distasteful chore to be performed with reluctance and bragged about afterward in the village. Consequently, the happiness she enjoyed came through the glad performance of the duty she willingly undertook.

BEYOND THE VISIBLE

Whereas our story thus far has been concerned with the plight of two widows and the commanding presence of Boaz, we will miss the whole point of this short book if we neglect to see God's hand at work behind the scenes. In the Law he pledged himself to be the Defender and Sustainer of widows and orphans. He called himself their Helper and Supporter (Pss. 68:5–6*a*; 146:9). He promised to visit retribution and the severest of penalties on those who defrauded and oppressed them (Ps. 94:6–11; Ezek. 22:7; Mal. 3:5).[3]

In caring for the needs of widows and orphans, God chose to work through people. The Israelites were to be his instruments in providing for them (Deut. 14:29), and the leaders were to be responsible for defending them (Isa. 1:17, 23). In our story, Boaz was the one through whom the Lord worked in order to alleviate Naomi and Ruth's privation (cf. Gal. 6:10).

RUTH 2:18–23

BREAD-AND-BUTTER ISSUES

Chapter 4 concluded with Ruth beating out the barley she had gleaned. As we take up the narrative once more, she returns to the village and shows Naomi what she has.

> And Ruth gleaned in the field until evening and beat out what she had gleaned, and it was about an ephah of barley.[4] And she took it up and went to the city. And her mother-in-law saw[5] what she had gleaned; and Ruth [also] brought out and gave to Naomi what remained [of the parched corn and vinegar] after she had eaten her fill[6] (2:17–18).

The scene is not too difficult to imagine. Ruth has worked hard all day. With a sense of satisfaction she beats out the grain into a shawl and carries it up the path to the city. We have no way of knowing who sees her, hot and tired from her exertion, as she enters Bethlehem and walks down the lanes that lead to Naomi's humble cottage.

Naomi too has spent a busy day. She completes whatever cleaning remains to be done, obtains some straw for bedding, and now waits for Ruth to return. She probably hears some of the other harvesters as they walk down the street, and it would be natural for her to feel anxious over Ruth. Where is she? Why hasn't she come? Has something happened to her?

At last Naomi hears Ruth approaching. Hardly knowing what to expect, she opens the door to let her in. As Ruth moves in through the doorway with her shawl filled with barley, she makes her way to the rough-hewn table in the center of the room. Her burden is a heavy one. She then opens her shawl and shows Naomi what she has gleaned. The text also tells us that Ruth gives to her mother-in-law some of the food Boaz had given her during the noon meal.

Evidence of Ruth's earlier hunger may be found in the fact that she ate her fill of the food Boaz served to her. We don't know when she and Naomi had their last meal, and the exertion of the morning may well have sapped her strength. There is also subtle evidence in the text to indicate that Naomi likewise is ravenous. Without being disrespectful, one gains the impression from Naomi's conversations (see 1:8–9, 11–13; 2:19) that she was an exuberant kind of woman. She appears to be effervescent and talkative—the kind of person you enjoy having about the house because she is always in good spirits. The text, however, does not contain any word of surprise from Naomi until *after* she eats Ruth's "leftovers."

RUTH 2:18–23

The *New American Standard Bible* translates verse 19*a* as follows:

Her mother-in-law *then* said to her, "Where did you glean today and where did you work?[7] May he who took notice of you be blessed"[8] [italics added].

If our sensitivity to the subtleties of the text has led us to the right conclusion, then we may safely say that it was only after Naomi's hunger was satisfied, when her spirits were revived, that her curiosity asserted itself. Her question, "Where did you glean today and where did you work?" is an example of Hebrew poetic parallelism. This, in itself, is indicative of an exuberant spirit. Under normal circumstances Naomi was evidently a person who loved life and whose cheerful disposition caused people to like her. And considering, too, her obvious interest in and concern for other people, it is not hard to see why she endeared herself to her daughter-in-law.

All of this was underscored by Naomi's next remark, "May he be blessed who took notice of you." The verb (*bārak*, "to bless," occurs about 330 times in the Bible. It was first used of God's blessing of the creation (cf. Gen. 1:22, 28; see also 9:1; 12:2–3; etc.). It represented the essence of goodness and stood in stark contrast to heathenism where power resided in the ability to curse (or bring evil upon) another.

The very fact that Naomi invoked happiness on their unnamed benefactor showed her basic disposition, which was characterized by godliness and an absence of selfishness. Dr. Samuel Cox wrote: "We are made to feel that we are with those in whom piety is an active and ruling power. Any woman, however selfish or godless, might have been as surprised and glad as Naomi was at this unexpected turn of fortune. But she, before even her question can be answered, is moved simply by the manifest happiness of Ruth in the abundance of her gleanings and 'blesses' the man who has given Ruth this happiness. For this she does not need to know who he is."[9]

SHARED VALUES

Ruth too reveals a guileless spirit. We read, "And she told her mother-in-law with whom she had worked, and she said, 'The name of the man with whom I worked today[10] [is] Boaz'" (2:19*b*).

Ruth's response to Naomi's questions is clear and direct. She is quite unaware of the fact that Boaz is a relative of her late father-in-law and has not the faintest hint of the role Boaz will play in her future. Furthermore, the innocent way in which she mentions Boaz's name shows that she has no idea of the dramatic import of her words. As Edward Campbell has pointed out, "The audience [listening to the story of Ruth gleaning in the field of Boaz] has known all along, but the dramatic suspense lies with the recognition that Naomi has not."[11] To her ears, the name of Boaz comes as a complete surprise.

With the mention of Boaz's name, Naomi apparently begins to see the hand of the Lord in the affairs of the day. She exclaims, "'Blessed be he of *Yahweh* who has not forsaken his kindness with the living[12] and with the dead.' And Naomi said to Ruth, 'The man [is] near [of kin] to us; he [is] one of our redeemers'" (2:20).

Naomi seems at once to grasp the significance of her young relative's kindness. She may have experienced one of those situations in life when a person senses something intuitively ahead of her ability to express it. In any event, she bursts forth into praise once more.

Naomi's words, however, pose an interpretative problem for us. She first gave thanks for Boaz, "Blessed be he of *Yahweh,*" and with a deep sense of gratitude recognized his kindness to her and Ruth. She then went on to say, "who has not forsaken his kindness . . ." and we at first are inclined to take the *who* as referring to Boaz. Leon Morris alerted us to the fact that "the whole drift of the passage shows that Naomi is thinking of God (cf. Gen. 24:27)."[13] This being the case, we have underscored for us Naomi's recognition of God's grace. *He* had not forsaken them nor their family.

Samuel Cox summarized Naomi's experience for us.

If we would enter into the force of this outburst of praise, we must remember that Naomi had lost her faith—not in God, indeed, but in the good will of God for her. She had thought that He was turned to be her foe, and the foe of the husband and sons who had been snatched from her by a premature death. They were dead because they had sinned in forsaking the land of the Covenant. She was bereaved, forsaken, "empty," because she had shared their sin. So, at least, she had conceived. But now, in the wonderful Providence which had led Ruth to find a friend in her valiant and wealthy kinsman, she [sees] proof that God had not wholly abandoned her, that He had not left off His kindness whether to her or to the beloved dead. No one who has witnessed such a [reversion] from spiritual despair to renewed hope in the Divine goodness and compassion will marvel at the ecstasy which breathes in Naomi's words. Rather, he will be sure that it would be long before she could recover her composure, and listen to what Ruth had still to tell; he will feel that in this brief exclamation of praise we have, compressed into a single sentence, the substance of many heartfelt thanksgivings.[14]

SEED THOUGHTS

Ruth's nonchalant mention of Boaz's name sparks Naomi's thought processes. Could her daughter-in-law's chance meeting with Boaz be the prelude to a long-term solution to their problem? The abundance of barley that Ruth has brought home might indicate Boaz's initial interest in her; but problems stand in the way of Boaz's exercising of the right of redemption, and so Naomi contents herself with saying to Ruth, "The man [is] near [of kin] to us; he [is] one of our *gō'ēlim* (redeemers)."

The word *gō'ēl*, "redeemer," needs some explanation.[15] A *gō'ēl* was a member of the family, sometimes a father, but more often a brother, on whom the duty of "redeeming" property (Lev. 25:23–28),[16] persons (Lev. 25:47–55),[17] or "blood vengeance"—the redressing of a wrong done by a member of the family (Num. 35:12, 19, 21, 24, 27; Deut. 19:6, 12; Josh. 20:3, 5, 9; etc.)[18]—devolved. Boaz, by being a relative of Elimelech, was one of their redeemers.

Associated with the duties of a *gō'ēl* was levirate marriage. In Ruth 1:11–13, Naomi makes reference to this ancient Hebrew custom.[19] The custom existed among the Hebrews before the giving of the Law (cf. Gen. 38:8) and involved the marriage of a man to his deceased brother's widow (in the event of his brother dying childless). Later on, the custom was given the sanction of Mosaic legislation (Deut. 25:5–10). For a brother to care for a sister-in-law and raise up a child to bear the name of the deceased and inherit his estate was regarded as *an act of love.*

Because Boaz is related to Elimelech, Naomi refers to him as "one of our close relatives"—one who might perform the duty of *gō'ēl.* The wheels of her mind are already turning, and she is hopeful that he will exercise the right of redemption on their behalf.[20] She hopes that because she is beyond childbearing age Boaz may be prepared to marry Ruth instead. Such a marriage would be unprecedented in the history of her people. It would necessitate that Boaz act in the *spirit* of the law, rather than adhere to its letter.

RUTH 2:18–23

TIMELY COUNSEL

Naomi does not become so preoccupied with her plans that she fails to listen to what Ruth is saying. This is a common problem and results in a breakdown of communication within many homes. Naomi listens to all that Ruth says. She even picks up on a small item that Ruth "dropped" in her recounting of the day's events, and that becomes the basis of her heartfelt counsel, as the text indicates:

And Ruth the Moabitess[21] said, "And he surely said to me, 'You shall stay close by the young men[22] whom I have [i.e., who work for me] until they have completed the whole harvest which I have [i.e., all my fields, both barley and wheat].'"

And Naomi said to Ruth, her daughter-in-law, "[It is] good, my daughter, that you go out with his young women, so that [men] will not attack[23] you in another field" (2:21–22).

The situation these verses describe is not hard to understand. Naomi is concerned about Ruth's safety. She is fearful lest someone take advantage of her and therefore stresses the importance of Ruth's remaining close to Boaz's young women.

Ruth is teachable. She listens to all that Naomi has to say. The inspired writer then concluded this portion of his account with the following summary:

And Ruth stayed close to Boaz's young women until the completion of the barley harvest and the wheat harvest[24]; and she lived with her mother-in-law (2:23).

FOOD FOR THOUGHT

As we review these verses, we learn several important lessons:

- The tensions of life should in no way lessen the satisfaction we receive from doing our appointed task.
- The encouragement we receive from the Lord should reinforce our commitment to him and his will for us.
- In all things we should exhibit a teachable spirit.

The Matter of Tension

The "Royal Preacher" of Ecclesiastes spent time considering the plight of man on the earth (i.e., "under the sun"). He concluded that, with all the vexations and inequities of life, and considering man's common end (the grave), "There is nothing better for a man than that he should make his soul enjoy the good of his labor." Then he added, "This also I saw, that it was from the hand of God" (Eccles. 2:24).

We are often caught up in tensions that rob us of our peace and deprive us of our happiness. We are subject to exploitation by others, endure unwarranted criticism, and face the pressures of competition from our colleagues. In recommending that his readers develop a spirit of contentment that will ease these tensions, Solomon suggested, "Better a handful [of bread] with quietness, than both hands full with travail and vexation of spirit" (Eccles. 4:6). His counsel was aimed at reducing stress and enabling those who will heed his advice to live happier, more contented lives.

For some people a certain amount of tension leads to productivity. They are reactive by nature, generally leave things to the last minute, and work best under pressure. They are not easy to live with or work for, and their personality bent deprives them of much of the happiness they could otherwise enjoy.

Others are caught up on the treadmill of more money, more possessions, more things. The pressure they feel to produce more, acquire more, and hoard more develops tensions that result in high blood pressure, sleeplessness, irritability, poor interpersonal relations, and a variety of physiological problems.

The evident ability of Ruth to cope with the pressure of providing for herself and Naomi, and Naomi's evident ability to exhibit gratitude and enjoy Ruth's company, model for us the way they overcame the tensions that would naturally be caused by their situation.

The antidote to worry is trust. Naomi had only recently returned to the place of blessing. Her trust was in the Lord. He assured her of his favor by blessing Ruth's efforts. And out of a heart filled with gratitude, she praised him for his goodness to her (2:20).

This Thing Called Confidence

The tangible evidence of God's love and favor toward her and Ruth gave Naomi confidence as together they faced the future. Their problems remained. They still were penniless, but Naomi's former despondency (cf. 1:11–14, 20–21) had now turned to a glad assurance. She therefore praised God that he had not forsaken his ḥeseḏ ("loving-kindness") to her or her husband.

RUTH 2:18–23

Confidence, in the biblical sense, is more than PMA—a positive mental attitude. It comes from a heart that is right with God. Confident people perceive how he reinforces their faith and trust and therefore gladly commit to him their tomorrows.

The evidences of God's grace toward us may come from a variety of sources: his Word, circumstances, or through a friend.

Some years ago I was visiting in a city when a friend of mine asked if I would visit one of his parishioners who was in the hospital awaiting surgery for the fusing of two vertebrae. Her husband had recently deserted her, and she felt very alone in the world. In addition, all my friend's efforts had failed to lift her spirits.

When I entered that hospital room and introduced myself, I did not find a woman in need of counsel or encouragement. She had been reading the Book of Psalms and had been led by David's example to place herself and her tomorrows entirely in God's hands. This included the outcome of the surgery the next day and the three full months of convalescence that would follow. Her appropriation of encouragement offered her in the Word of God was sufficient to sustain her.

Sometimes God uses circumstances as a means of encouraging us. These may be the result of prayer or may be connected with the more mundane things of life, like having our car start when it is minus twenty degrees outside, having schedules somehow adjust to meet our needs, or having a "chance" encounter result in the solution of a dilemma. When these things happen, we should see God's hand behind the temporal circumstance and be appropriately thankful.

As God's agents on the earth, we can also bring encouragement to others. The Lord may place us in situations whereby we can bring help or blessing to a needy soul.

Samuel Cox expressed it this way:

> When we consider how potent our kindness may be in quickening the sense of God's kindness and compassion in a neighbour's heart, and how potent, therefore, our lack of kindness and compassion may be, in inducing or confirming a neighbour's despair, we may well tremble at the responsibility which, at any moment, may fall on us. It was not until Naomi arrived in Bethlehem, and saw her neighbours indifferent and apathetic, however curious and inquisitive they were, that she concluded herself to be shut out from the mercy of God. It was only when Boaz showed a little kindness to her daughter—such a kind-

RUTH 2:18–23

ness as we may show a neighbour any day—that she felt the door of
mercy was once more thrown open to her.[25]

The importance of displaying godly kindness places a solemn
responsibility on each one of us.

Teachable Spirit

The satisfied and committed spirit will also be teachable. Over
and over again Ruth willingly subordinates herself to her mother-in-
law. She heeds Naomi's counsel and never complains about her
advice. And in our next chapter, we will have a further illustration of
Ruth's teachable spirit.

Being teachable is indispensable to our personal growth. Those
who "know everything" and cannot be taught anything demonstrate
by their attitude their immaturity and resistance to growth.

The truth did not threaten Ruth, and she gladly accepted the
counsel given her (cf. 2:8–9, 22). As a new convert, Ruth was learn-
ing about the customs as well as the culture of God's people. She
did not expect utopia and took seriously Naomi's warning that she
might be sexually molested if she went to some other field.

Ruth also had a mature attitude. She was not a wide-eyed "Pol-
lyanna" believing that now that she had come to trust "under *Yahweh's* wings" (2:12) everything would be perfect. Furthermore, she
did not regard Naomi's warning as needless and reply, "Don't worry;
I know how to look after myself." Instead, she accepted Naomi's
words in the spirit in which they were given and incorporated all
that she saw and heard as a part of the growth experiences of life.

From Ruth's example, we learn that through our teachableness in
little things we prepare ourselves (as Ruth did) for the momentous
experiences of life. These experiences only come when we are prepared for them.

6 | MOVED BY LOVE

Ruth
3:1–13

How would you describe *love*?

Imagine that you are on a television game show and have been asked to write down your view of love in twenty-five words or less. What would you say?

When pushed for some profound insights into the nature of love, certain celebrities, who had the opportunity to respond to the question, said:

- Love is the fairest flower that blooms in God's garden.
- Love is a ticklish sensation around the heart that can't be scratched.
- Love is like a vaccination. When it takes hold you don't have to be told.
- Of all human passions love is the strongest, for it attacks simultaneously the head, the heart, and the senses.
- Love makes a fellow feel funny and act stupid.

Now, in all candor, such verbiage does not aid our understanding of love.

To the high-school student, love is a steamy session on the backseat of a car. To a Hollywood producer, it is a temporary relationship satisfying the urge of the moment, with television viewers always aware that next week the encounter will be with someone else. To the fellow in the office with a wife and three children at home, it is often identified with a quiet weekend somewhere with his wife so that they can recapture the mystery of their early romance. To the single career woman, it is the elusive promise of companionship that forever seems to escape her. To the inveterate watcher of afternoon television soap operas or the effervescent reader of romantic novels, it is the perpetuation of "puppy love" without the threat of it leading to a "dog's life."

Our view of love tends to reflect our individual personalities, and to be an expression of our own needs and desires. It is, therefore, often highly subjective.

Our lack of clarity over what constitutes real love has led some clinicians to try to objectively analyze it. After extensive research, the famous psychiatrist, Dr. Henry Stack Sullivan, described love in the following cautious terms: "When a person's care and concern for another is as great as his care and concern for himself, then a state of love may be said to exist."[1]

This definition bears close resemblance to Matthew 22:39. What Sullivan's definition left out was the first prerequisite, the vertical dimension with a loving God (v. 37), on which the horizontal depends. For love, to be sustaining, must be more than the measure of our concern for ourselves.

From a biblical point of view, *love is seen in our desire for the highest good in the one loved, even to the point of self-sacrifice.* Only a definition such as this can satisfy the demands of Scriptural passages like John 3:16 and 15:13.

UNCERTAIN FUTURE

As we examine Ruth 3, we find three illustrations of mature love. First, there was Naomi. Acting out of a heart filled with love for Ruth, she desired to see her happily married, comfortably ensconced in a home, and able to enjoy the blessings of a husband's companionship and protection. To accomplish this, Naomi devised a plan which, if successful, would see Ruth happily united to a noble man while she herself may have to endure a lonely, poverty-stricken old age.

The second illustration of mature love was Ruth. She was aware of Naomi's motives and, in carrying out Naomi's plan, had every intention of ensuring Naomi's protection. Boaz realized this and praised her: "May you be blessed of *Yahweh,* my daughter. You have shown in this last kindness [to Naomi, in contracting a marriage within the family of Elimelech] to be better than the first [when you left your homeland in order to care for your mother-in-law], for you have not sought for marriage by going after the young men, whether poor or rich" (3:10).

Finally, Boaz illustrated his genuine love for the family of his deceased relative, Elimelech, by expressing his willingness to provide for both Naomi and Ruth (cf. 4:9–10). As Dr. Leggett has pointed out in his book, *Levirate and Goel Institutions in the Old Testament,* "It is important to recognize that the levirate duty entailed a sacrifice of love." Then, commenting on Boaz's words in Ruth 4:10, he emphasized the selflessness of the "redeemer" who, in perpetuating the "name of the dead in his inheritance," performed an act of love that never could be repaid.[2]

With these thoughts in mind, let us observe the outworking of mature love in the relationships of Naomi, Ruth, and Boaz.

> And Naomi, Ruth's mother-in-law, said to her, "My daughter, have I not been seeking[3] rest[4] for you, that it may be well with you? And now, is not Boaz of our kindred,[5] with whose young women you have been? Behold, he [is] winnowing barley [at] the threshing floor[6] tonight.[7] Now you shall wash and anoint yourself,[8] and put on your garments,[9] and go down[10] to the threshing floor; [but] do not let yourself be known to the man[11] until after he has finished eating and drinking. And it shall be, when he lies down that you shall know [i.e., take note of] the place where he lies down, and you shall go in and uncover his feet,[12] and lie down. And he will tell you what you are to do." And Ruth said to her, "All that you say, I will do." And she went down to the threshing floor and did according to all that her mother-in-law [had] commanded her (3:1–6).

A Respectable Haven

Naomi is concerned about her daughter-in-law. She desires to see Ruth married. The text implies that she has been thinking seriously about how to accomplish this. Now as she shares her plan with Ruth, we become aware of her loving concern for her daughter-in-law.

Some commentators have severely criticized Naomi for suggesting that Ruth go to the threshing floor outside Bethlehem at night and ask Boaz to marry her. So defensive have some become that they have overlooked the positive teaching of the passage.

Naomi desires only what is best for Ruth. A widow's lot was a hard one, and her livelihood was precarious.[13] It will be many long months before the next harvest. Naomi is anxious for her daughter-in-law's safety. She desires for Ruth that security and blessing, protection and companionship, that stem from the union of a good man and a good woman.

Naomi again uses the word *rest* to describe this union. *Mānôh,* here translated "rest," implied more than a home. It has inherent within it the idea of mutual love, acceptance, a cessation from striving to attain something. It was used in some contexts of the complete envelopment or permeation of someone by something, evoking a sense of peace or quietness—hence the use of the word *rest.* It is this atmosphere of mutual love and respect and security that Naomi desires for Ruth, and marriage (then, as now) is such a haven for a woman.

Since Ruth had first mentioned Boaz's kindness to her (see 2:19), Naomi has had time to watch Boaz. She has not seen him in more than a decade, and she wonders if he will be a suitable husband for Ruth. Apparently what she has observed impresses her. Boaz appears to be one of those rare individuals who is motivated by principles, not expediency; he wants to do what is right regardless of personal preference or convenience. Furthermore, he has demonstrated that he can be trusted with the welfare of another. All of this commends him to her.

Having checked everything carefully, Naomi now makes her proposal to Ruth. Her words are full of kindness: "My daughter, have I not been seeking rest for you?" (3:1). This is a Hebraism, stating a positive fact with a question. Naomi is also reassuring. She reminds Ruth of Boaz's kindnesses to her and the fact that she has spent the past six weeks in the company of his maids. Her plan, though, is not without its difficulties. It will require prompt action, for (and this fact may only now have come to her attention) Boaz will be threshing grain that night. It will also require courage, for Ruth will need to go to the threshing floor at night and there ask Boaz to marry her.

For Naomi's plan to succeed, it will require the "help of the Almighty." As Dr. Moshe Weinfeld has said, this natural story, "in which everything moves by human agents and, as it were, without divine interference, actually serves as a testimony for the wondrous ways in which God leads men [generically speaking] toward His destiny. . . . The occurrences which look like a chain of natural happenings evolving one from the other, reveal themselves in the end as the outcome of God's plan."[14]

RUTH 3:1–13

Although Naomi is unaware of the Lord's hand in these matters, she is satisfied that Boaz is a man who can be trusted with Ruth's safety. She therefore recommends that Ruth bathe and anoint herself with perfume, put on her clothes, and go down to the threshing floor. After Boaz retires, she is to uncover his feet and lie down next to him. When he awakens, she is to ask him to marry her.

Naomi is confident that Boaz and Ruth will conduct themselves with due circumspection. As Dr. Morris has pointed out, "The fact that [Naomi] was prepared to urge this course on Ruth is the measure of her trust in both participants."[15] Another couple, less mature in themselves and less committed to doing what is right, might not prove trustworthy in a similar situation.

Naomi wisely cautions Ruth. Immoral practices associated with fertility rites were practiced on pagan threshing floors. Ruth, therefore, will need to be careful as well as discreet, and "not make herself known" to Boaz until well after dark when everyone else is asleep.

The Local Setting

Threshing floors in these times were frequently situated in the immediate vicinity of the harvest field. A raised, level area was used, and the floor was packed down hard so as to provide a durable surface. The grain was then placed in a pile on the floor and a heavy, flat slab of rock was sometimes dragged over it by oxen.

After the threshers had initially separated the grain from the stalk and chaff, they threw it with a fork into the air against a strong wind. The heavier grain would fall to the ground, but the remaining lighter stalk and chaff would be blown to the end of the threshing floor where a slow fire would be burning (cf. Matt. 3:12).

Evenings were normally chosen for this kind of work, perhaps because the wind blew more steadily from one direction. In any event, the owner or foreman would usually sleep on the threshing floor with his men in order to protect his harvest from robbers.

Understanding how farmers harvested their grain, Naomi gives Ruth some precise instructions.

And Ruth went down to the grain floor and did according to all[16] that her mother-in-law had commanded her.[17] And Boaz ate and drank,[18] and his heart [felt] good;[19] and he went to lie down at the end of the

RUTH 3:1–13

heap [of grain].[20] And Ruth came in quietly[21] and uncovered his feet[22] and lay down. And it came to pass [lit., and it was], in the middle of the night,[23] that the man trembled[24] and turned himself, and behold, a woman[25] [was] lying at his feet. And he said, "Who are you?"[26] and she said, "I [am] Ruth, your handmaid;[27] spread your wing[28] over your handmaid, for you [are] a redeemer."[29] And Boaz said, "Blessed[30] [be] you of *Yahweh,* my daughter, you have done well [in that] your kindness in the end [is] more than at the beginning,[31] and you have not gone after the young men,[32] either poor or rich. And now, my daughter,[33] do not fear; all that you say I will do for you, for all the gate[34] of my people knows that you are a woman of valor [i.e., worth].[35] And now, surely [it is] true that I [am] a redeemer,[36] but also there is a redeemer nearer than I.[37] Stay [here] tonight,[38] and it shall be in the morning, if he will redeem you, good; he will redeem [you];[39] and if he is not pleased[40] to redeem you, then, as *Yahweh* lives,[41] I will redeem you. Lie down until the morning" (3:6–13).

These verses describe the events clearly and concisely. They are eloquent in their simplicity. Mention of another redeemer nearer of kin than Boaz holds the listener's attention. Inwardly there is a desire to see Boaz and Ruth together.

CLIMAX OF THE HARVEST

Boaz and his men sit around the fire eating and drinking, and then lie down on the floor for the night. Boaz takes his place near the heap of grain while his men probably choose places to rest at the end of the threshing floor near the fire.

In the light of the flickering flame, Ruth takes note of where Boaz lies down. When everyone is asleep and the fire has died to little more than glowing embers, she creeps quietly to the place where he is sleeping. Then, uncovering his feet so that he will awaken when they become cold, she lies down and waits.

Some Bible scholars believe that Ruth's "uncovering of Boaz's feet" is a euphemism for sexual intercourse. As we shall find later in this chapter, such a view is unfounded.

IMPORTANT PRINCIPLES

Ruth's actions illustrate for us certain important biblical principles:

RUTH 3:1–13

- For the provision of God's Word to be fulfilled, the believer must first be completely identified with the Lord and his cause (see 1:16; cf. Matt. 6:33).
- The promises of God's Word must be claimed by faith.

Ruth met the first of these conditions when she turned her back on her home, her people, and her former manner of life, and in words of exquisite beauty forever identified herself with Naomi, her people, and her God (cf. 2:12).

In claiming the fulfillment of the provisions of the covenant (cf. Deut. 25:5–10), Ruth went down to the threshing floor. Her faith was seen in her belief in a possibility against all probabilities. Hers was not a faddish faith, for such can be as dangerous as faith that is false. Rather it was a faith that was devoid of presumption and relied solely on what the Lord himself had communicated to his people. As such, it was, to quote Martin Luther, "a living, daring confidence in God's grace" and his power to work out in her experience that which was, from man's point-of-view, impossible.

So we see that Ruth met two important criteria for receiving God's blessing: (1) She had fulfilled the conditions of the covenant (note 1:16*b*), and (2) she was therefore in a position to claim its blessings.

For us these twin truths mean (1) living in obedience to God's revealed will, and (2) then claiming by faith the blessings of his manifold provision for us (cf. 2 Pet. 1:4, KJV).

In Ruth's case, she lived obediently under the law. First, her submission to it was not the result of some legalistic imperative but rather the response of an enlightened person to the grace of God. Second, in claiming the benefits of God's covenant, she acted in faith, not knowing how matters would turn out.

Many of us fail on one of these points. On some occasions we may not have fulfilled the conditions before we claim the promise. Such acts, therefore, are presumptuous. At other times, when we have done all that God requires of us, we may wait patiently for the fulfillment of our prayers, not realizing that God expects us to claim his promised blessing. Fulfilling the conditions must precede the claiming of the promise, and the claiming of the promise must demonstrate the reality of our faith.

In claiming the promise, Ruth's attitude was seen to be humble and discreet. She took appropriate precautions to ensure her safety;

and when she stated her request, it was brief, pointed, and picturesque. She was sincere, and Boaz responded with positive
assurance.

NAOMI'S CHOICE

Boaz has been unaware of Naomi's plans. His introduction to
them comes suddenly when he awakens in the middle of the night to
find a woman lying at his feet. D.B. MacDonald described his mature
reaction: "Boaz is shown quietly handling the situation like a gentle-
man, and not either as an old fool or a village lout. He may be
countrified but he has dignity and restraint."[42]

On hearing Ruth's plea, Boaz readily accedes to her request. He
also praises her for her loyalty to her mother-in-law. Then he explains that, while he is indeed a near relative, there is one nearer of
kin to Elimelech than he (3:12). This statement, Robert Watson believed, explained why Boaz had not done more for Naomi and Ruth
following their return from Moab. Boaz apparently did all he could
to aid them, but within the bounds of social custom and in a way
that would not cause Elimelech's "nearer kinsman" to take offense
or lose face.[43]

With the assurance that he will do all he can to see that Ruth is
taken care of, Boaz instructs her to lie down with him until morning
(3:13).

FLESHLY INDULGENCE?

Many commentators have believed that Boaz had sexual relations
with Ruth that night. They maintained that in this way he pledged
himself to marry her. Others believed that this was part of Naomi's
plan and that, after seducing Ruth, he felt obligated to redeem her.

The biblical writer chose his words carefully, and in his use of
specific terms ruled out all possibility of moral impropriety. The
Hebrew word *lûn* "to pass the night" denoted simply the passage of
time and did not imply anything about the manner in which time
was spent. If Boaz and Ruth had engaged in sexual relations on the
threshing floor, then *šākab* "to lie [together], to sleep [together]"
would have been used. *Lûn* is a word devoid of sexual connotations.

Naomi's confidence in Boaz's character proved fully justified. He
and Ruth both could regulate their conduct without being ruled by
their passions.[44]

RUTH 3:1–13

We make a grave mistake, however, if we think of Boaz and Ruth as following mechanically a well-rehearsed plot without being deeply involved in the dynamics of what was taking place. They were people with emotions as we are and felt keenly the dramatic changes that the decision on the threshing floor would make in their lives.

The Emotion Factor

As Ruth lies on the floor at Boaz's feet, she probably wonders whether Elimelech's "nearer relative" will exercise his option and take her as his concubine[45] or give Boaz the right to marry her. And how will she handle the additional responsibilities of a wife and still care for her mother-in-law? Naomi's proposal has given her no time to prepare for the new role that will soon be hers. And will she be able to bear a child? Ten years of marriage to Mahlon fails to produce any offspring.

And what of Boaz? Certainly sleep for him is out of the question. What is revealed in Ruth 4 shows that he must have worked out a careful plan of action. It includes protecting the rights of his kinsman by making him aware of the issues (cf. 4:3–4), while at the same time giving him the opportunity to decline gracefully if he feels that redeeming Ruth will be too great a burden. Boaz's thoughts are also of Elimelech, for he plans to care for Naomi as well. This will place him under a heavy financial burden. And *if* his plan is successful, *if* redeeming Ruth does become a reality. . . . With this he carefully rehearses to himself what he will say before the elders and the people of the city (cf. 4:9–10).

THE HAPPINESS QUOTIENT

Before leaving this passage, we should reflect on the ways in which love may be allowed to permeate our relationships.

The Personal Dynamic

First of all, Ruth and Naomi conversed freely, openly, and naturally. They had time for each other. They had fellowship together. Ruth shared with Naomi the events of the day, and Naomi shared with Ruth her counsel for the morrow (cf. 2:21–22; 3:1–5).

RUTH 3:1–13

In our day we have become obsessed with *doing* rather than *being*. We are consumed with meetings to attend and responsibilities to assume. Church, PTA, civic functions, social gatherings, and Little League are only some of the activities that keep us on the treadmill. We seldom have leisure time to sit down and talk with those whom we love, share our experiences, discuss our mutual interests, and be supportive of one another.

Accompanying our preoccupation with things has come an inability to be able to listen to what others are saying. This is frequently linked with a corresponding inability to sense how others feel. Husbands have forgotten how to truly empathize with their wives, and wives have forgotten how to be supportive of their husbands. As the deterioration of their union continues, the channels of communication become blocked. Each becomes intent on fulfilling his or her own unmet needs. And as time goes by, while they may continue to share the same address, the romance disappears from their relationship. They are more and more like strangers living under the same roof.

The same problem frequently is carried over into the relationship of parents with their children. Building a quality relationship takes time and effort and many parents drift into patterns of behavior in which trite answers and superficial comments have replaced mature conversation. The result is that, with their thoughts and feelings centering more and more on themselves, they frequently do not heed the signals for help from their children.[46]

The relationship of Naomi and Ruth provides a pattern of fellowship and interaction and an illustration of how relational problems can be solved. Their lives were not free from anxiety, but their priorities were in order. They took time each day in a relaxed, unstructured way, to communicate with each other. And as they did so, their love for one another was strengthened.

Formula for Happiness

A second principle, which is closely related to making time to share our feelings openly and honestly and to talk about the events of the day, concerns happiness within a marriage and the type of people who should marry. Marriage should only be entered into by those who are mature and share common beliefs, values, and goals; who are able to maintain a lasting relationship with the person whom they choose to marry; and who demonstrate their capacity to enjoy life.

By far the commonest cause of marital problems is the immaturity of one or both spouses.[47]

In Genesis 2:24 God gave us the basis for marital union. A man must be prepared to "leave his father and mother" (implying his physical, intellectual, moral, and emotional maturity), and "cleave to his wife" (stressing the importance of unity arising out of their shared beliefs, values, and goals); and "the two of them becoming one flesh" (underscoring the need for sexual compatibility). Furthermore, in verse 25, God revealed that Adam and Eve were "naked and unashamed." This implied a perfect acceptance of each other's physiological and psychological differences. Anything less than personal maturity, the development of true unity, the cultivation of sexual compatibility, and the free acceptance of each other's individuality, is an intimation of potential difficulty in a marriage.

From our study of Ruth 1–3, we know that Boaz and Ruth were mature in themselves and brought to their marriage a sense of maturity. Their relationship was free from narcissistic tensions that would tend to redirect the focus of their relationship from each other to themselves. Boaz and Ruth were inwardly secure, regardless of their outward situation. They both possessed qualities of character that were mutually attractive. Furthermore, their maturity was seen in their personal restraint. They were able to control themselves in what might have become a highly compromising situation, and yet each felt free later on to express their love in appropriate ways. They were an ideal couple, with all the potential for developing a lasting, mutually satisfying relationship.

Happiness Is Homemade

A final ingredient for a happy marriage is the ability to enjoy life. Whether a person has much or little in terms of temporal prosperity, the capacity to take delight in what otherwise might be mundane and invest even the commonplace with significance makes a world of difference to a relationship. Those who possess such an outlook are always fun to be with and seem to grow better (rather than older) with the passing of the years.

Boaz had an outgoing nature. In chapter 2 he cheerfully greeted the reapers, ate the noonday meal with them, and spoke kindly to a stranger. In chapter 3 he enjoyed the festivity of the harvest season and, as the text intimates, "his heart was 'good'" (3:7). And when he later took on the added responsibility of caring for Naomi and Ruth, we may be sure that his ability to enjoy life would be as full as ever.

Ruth, too, showed that she was at heart a happy person. She was fully in touch with her emotions, yet she never gave way to despondency. Her love and devotion to Naomi, her assertion in providing for her mother-in-law's physical needs, and her pleasant conversation each evening were all indicative of her cheerful, loving nature. And as she would soon be taken as Boaz's wife, and later on bear him a son, we may be sure that in the enjoyment of this "rest," she brought to the home and the responsibilities of motherhood a wise, gracious, and loving spirit.

All of this brings us to an important conclusion. Marriage, regardless of what contemporary voices may be saying about alternative life-styles, is the place where love finds its fullest expression and its greatest reward. Naomi realized this when she earnestly sought "rest" for Ruth. Different movements today are propagating different ideas about marriage. We are being told that conventional marriage is "restrictive," that traditional beliefs about marriage are as "outmoded as the horse and buggy," that being "just a housewife" programs a person for dependency, that couples who are "hooked on togetherness" will eventually find this to be "destructive of the marital relationship," and that only by breaking out of the marriage "trap" can a person be free to mature as an individual.[48]

These slanted terms do not describe marriage in the true sense of the word, but they have had an unsettling effect on many people. Such views, however, are not shared by everyone, as one letter to the editor of the *Saturday Review* made clear:

> I am hopelessly behind the times. I'm a housewife. That means I spend three hours a day cooking and cleaning. The rest of the time I read, dream, study, listen to records, and paint. And, oh yes, I take care of my baby, which for some completely illogical reason is the warmest, most satisfying experience I've ever had—next to making my husband feel that he couldn't be happy without me.[49]

This is the kind of situation Naomi desired for Ruth, and it still holds greater promise of satisfaction for both husband and wife than any of the alternatives that have been suggested in recent years.

RUTH 3:1–13

7 DEEDS OF THE RIGHTEOUS

Ruth
3:14–4:6

Dr. Richard Selzer, in describing an incident that took place during his medical internship, illustrated the need for sensitivity.

One day, while passing the bulletin board of the hospital, he saw a notice. It advised those on the staff that Dr. Yashi Dhonden, an eminent Tibetan physician, would make his rounds on a particular morning.

Such an opportunity was not to be missed, and on the morning in question, Dr. Selzer joined the clutch of whitecoats a little before 6:00 A.M. and waited. At precisely six o'clock Dr. Dhonden appeared. He was short, golden-skinned, rotund, and dressed in a sleeveless robe of saffron and maroon. He was clean-shaven.

Yashi Dhonden bowed to his colleagues as he entered. He then asked to see the patient who had been selected for examination. The patient, of course, had been awakened a short time before, advised of what was going to take place, and had been asked for a fresh specimen of urine.

On entering the patient's room, Dr. Dhonden noticed her spirit of compliance—the attitude of resignation that frequently is shown by a chronically ill person. He, however, said nothing. Instead, he walked to the bed and for a long time gazed at her, yet not so as to cause embarrassment. No physical sign or obvious symptom gave him a clue as to the nature of her ailment. Then he took her hand in both of his and with his eyes closed felt her pulse. His concentration was obvious. His rapt attention made him oblivious to the passing of time.

At last he straightened, gently placed the woman's hand back on the bed, and stepped backward. Speaking through an interpreter he asked for the urine specimen. This he likewise examined. He then turned to leave.

Before Dr. Dhonden could pass through the door, the woman raised her head off the pillow and said, "Thank you, doctor." She evidently felt that this Asian physician understood her suffering.

Alone with the men of his profession, Yashi Dhonden gave his diagnosis. Little was lost through the interpreter. He spoke in pictures and symbols. He described winds coursing through the body of an unborn child and of currents breaking against barriers. Between the chambers of her heart, long before she was born, a "wind" had "blown open a gate" that must never be opened. Through this opening now charged the full "waters" of her bloodstream.

Without elaborate tests, X rays, or exploratory surgery, Dr. Dhonden had diagnosed congenital heart disease: an interventricular septal defect with resultant heart failure.[1]

SENSITIVE AND HONEST

In the same way that this Tibetan doctor was able to become vitally in tune with the patient's body and intimately aware of her condition, so we too should develop an unhurried understanding of what God is saying to us through his Word. This will not happen all at once, but each of us can develop the skills we need if we persevere.

In our present story, for example, we notice:

- the obvious empathy between Ruth and Boaz. Ruth sensed intuitively Boaz's concern about her being seen on the threshing floor and took the initiative by rising early "before one could recognize another" (3:14). Boaz sensed her concern. He approved of her action and said, "Let it not be known that a woman came to the threshing floor."
- God's evident involvement in the events that took place at the gate. Boaz had just made himself comfortable when *"behold, there is the very kinsman of whom he had spoken"* (4:1). The word *behold* might not arouse much interest on our part, but this device of drawing our attention to events as they are transpiring has been used repeatedly by the writer (2:4; 3:8; 4:1).

RUTH 3:14–4:6

- that the kinsman of Naomi was not named (4:1). This does not mean that neither Boaz nor the recorder of these events knew his name. Rather it implies that the writer used this tactful device so that descendants of the individual might not be offended. From our point of view, the unnamed kinsman passes off the page of Scripture and soon fades from our minds.

- the way in which Boaz graciously yet firmly took charge of the meeting at the gate ("Turn aside . . . sit down here" [v. 1]): the control of his own emotions, which was so evident in his timing (e.g., in not mentioning the reason for the meeting until he was ready); and the way in which he offered his relative a way to save face before the elders and all the people ("Buy [the field] before those sitting here . . . but if you will not redeem [the field], tell me . . . [and] I will redeem it" [v. 4]). All this pointed to the maturity and wisdom of the one whom Naomi had selected as the best husband for Ruth.

- clues to the motive of the unnamed kinsman. His intentions became apparent when we consider how readily he wished to add to his own estate ("I will redeem it" [v. 4]). However, when he learned that Ruth was also involved in the "purchase," he quickly changed his mind. This becomes very evident when we observe the repetition of "for" in verse 6 (*lî*, "for myself," contrasted with *lekā*, "for yourself").[2] Notice also the subtle stress of his words: "*I* cannot . . . lest *I* . . . *my* right . . . *I* cannot." He apparently was thinking only of himself.

NEW DAY DAWNING

With renewed sensitivity, therefore, we read Ruth 3:14–18:

And Ruth lay at his feet[3] until the morning, and she[4] arose before a man could discern his neighbor.[5] And Boaz said, "Do not let it be known that a [lit., the[6]] woman came to the threshing floor." And he said, "Give me the cloak which is on you, and hold on to it."[7] And Ruth kept hold on it, and he measured six [*seah*][8] of barley [into it] and laid it on her.[9] Then he[10] went into the city.

And Ruth came to her mother-in-law, and Naomi said, "How did things go, my daughter?" (lit., Who are you?).[11] And Ruth told her all that Boaz [lit., the man] had done to her. And she said, "He gave me these six [*seah*] of barley, for he said, 'You shall not go empty to your mother-in-law.'"[12] And Naomi said, "Sit, my daughter, until you shall know how [the] matter[13] falls [i.e., how everything turns out], for the man will not rest until he has completed the matter today."

SACRED VALUES

Being a woman of maturity and believing in the sanctity of marriage, Ruth lies at Boaz's feet (not by his side!) until the first blush of dawn on the Hebrew hills heralds the approach of a new day. Then, wishing to protect Boaz from any unnecessary scandal, she arises so as to leave the threshing floor before any of the men who have slept there become aware of her presence.

Boaz too arises. He is a righteous man, but he is also sufficiently in touch with the seamy side of human nature to know how readily those of the city will seize on a seeming indiscretion to tarnish his reputation and sully Ruth's character.

Such wisdom is not often found among generous large-hearted people. They frequently expect people to act toward them with the same magnanimity they show others, and their very honesty makes them vulnerable.

Boaz, therefore, serves as a good model of the wise person who is able to apply his insight to various situations. He understands that it is easier to prevent a problem than to solve it after it has arisen.

Tangible Commitment

In sending Ruth back to the city, Boaz takes care that she not return to Naomi empty-handed. He asks her to take off her mantle and hold one end of it. He then places in it six *seah* of barley. Because the quantity of barley is such that Ruth cannot satisfactorily lift it *and* adjust it for carrying, Boaz sets it on her. He then allows her to return to Naomi.

Two questions concern us: (1) Why does Boaz feel that it is necessary to send Naomi a gift? and (2) Is there anything significant in the fact that in Ruth 1:21 Naomi had complained of returning to Bethlehem "empty" and here Boaz says, "Do not return *empty* to your mother-in-law"?

In answering the first question, it seems as if this gift of barley is a pledge to Naomi, some tangible assurance, that he will indeed redeem her. As such, it serves to illustrate the generosity of a righteous man who was prepared to do more than the law required of him.

As far as the second question is concerned, the remainder of Naomi's situation serves to underscore the grace of God. He brought Naomi back to Judah stripped of her wealth and deprived of her family. Now in response to her renewed trust in him, he was in the process of making provision for her future needs. She would not know want or suffer privation again. And in time God would also give her a son (cf. 4:13*b* with vv. 15–17*a*).

A Bit of History

Bible translation history was made with verse 15. The Hebrew text reads, "And *he* [Boaz] went into the city." Most of our translations follow an emended text and have Ruth going to the city.

When the Authorized (King James) Version of the Bible was first published in 1611, the first edition followed the Masoretic (Hebrew) text. It became known as the "He" Bible. In the same year a second printing was called for, and in this edition the text was changed to read, "And *she* went in to the city." This printing became known as the "She" Bible.[14]

Scholars still are undecided as to which translation is to be preferred. The point fortunately is not of vital importance, but we have chosen to adhere to the reading of the Hebrew text. After filling Ruth's mantle with barley, Boaz went into the city. There he prepared for the events of the day. This left the writer free to conclude this chapter as it began, with Naomi and Ruth.

Learning to Trust God

Ruth returns to Naomi with the six measures of barley.[15] She shares with her mother-in-law all that has transpired during the night. Of concern to both women is whether or not the nearer kinsman will exercise the rights of a redeemer, buy the field, and marry Ruth.

Realizing that nothing is to be gained by fretfully pacing the floor, Naomi counsels Ruth to sit still and await the outcome of the events that will soon transpire at the city gate.

Such times of waiting frequently produce anxiety and are destructive of faith. It is hard to wait. Tension mounts and we feel that we should be *doing* something.

Naomi's recommendation to Ruth is based on her knowledge of Boaz's character. She knows him to be a person who is as good as

RUTH 3:14–4:6

his word. He is proactive and decisive. He will not rest until the issue
has been resolved. And because the whole affair ultimately rests in
God's hands, Ruth does not need to fret or become overly anxious.
Trust is the antidote to anxiety, and sitting still and waiting is the
best course of action for Ruth to follow.

A PROMISE TO KEEP

As the scene moves to the gate of the city, the writer stresses
Boaz's character:

> Then Boaz went up to the gate[16] and sat there; and behold the near
> kinsman [i.e., the close relative] of whom he had spoken was passing
> by.[17] And Boaz said to him, "Turn aside,[18] sit down here." And he
> turned aside and sat down. And Boaz took ten men of the elders of the
> city[19] and said, "Sit down here." And they sat down.
>
> And Boaz said to the near kinsman, "Naomi, who has returned from
> the fields of Moab, will sell[20] the portion of the field which [belonged]
> to our brother Elimelech. And I said, 'I will uncover your ear[21] [i.e.,
> inform you], saying, "Acquire it before those sitting [here] and before
> the elders of my people." If you will redeem [it], redeem [it]; but if he[22]
> will not redeem [it], tell me so that I may know; for there is no one
> apart from you to redeem [it], and I[23] [am] after you.'"
>
> And he said "I will redeem [it]."
>
> And Boaz said, "In the day of your acquiring[24] the field from the
> hand of Naomi, you must also acquire Ruth the Moabitess, the wife of
> the dead, to raise up the name of the dead on his inheritance."[25]
>
> And the near kinsman said, "I am not able to redeem [it] for myself,
> lest I ruin my own inheritance.[26] You redeem [it] for yourself; you
> [take] my right to redeem it, for I am not able to redeem [it]" (4:1–6).

Forgotten Faces

While Ruth and Naomi wait patiently at home, not knowing how
their future will be affected by the events of the day, Boaz goes up to
the gate through which the citizens will pass on their way to the
fields.

Just as he takes a seat within the wall, the close relative of Elimelech passes by. Boaz calls out to him, *pelônı 'alemônı,* signifying
that he has something of a legal nature to discuss with him. He
courteously asks his kinsman to take a seat and then impanels ten
trustworthy elders of the city. With everything ready, Boaz opens

RUTH 3:14–4:6

the proceedings by informing his relative of Naomi's decision to sell the portion of the field that belonged to Elimelech. He reminds his kinsman that his relationship to Elimelech is closer than Boaz's, but assures him of his willingness to purchase the land should the man not be in a position to do so.

The unnamed kinsman quickly agrees to buy the land. His "*I* will redeem it" is emphatic.

No Trade-offs

The subtle emphases of the Hebrew text have led different students of the Word to probe for the motivating force behind the kinsman's immediate willingness to buy Naomi's property.[27]

Although he could excuse himself from any form of levirate[28] (i.e., brother-in-law) responsibility on the grounds that Boaz's recommendation did not conform to the letter of the law (cf. Lev. 25:23–28), this kinsman tacitly admitted the legitimacy of Boaz's suggestion. The right of redemption was for the benefit of the poor. Did this *gō'ēl* stand to gain from the transaction?

The answer he gave seemed to point to his inherent selfishness. In Israel those who sold property had it restored to them at the year of Jubilee; but if they had a kinsman who would buy it back for them, it was to be purchased from the buyer and restored to the owner. In this way the property would always remain in the family and practical help was extended to those in need.

In Naomi's case, she was a widow, her sons were dead, and she was beyond childbearing years. To purchase the field from her would then mean that the land would become the property of the kinsman without any fear of it being bought back (i.e., redeemed) by any of Naomi's descendants.

This kinsman, therefore, could add to his present possessions with no legal way of Naomi ever recovering the land.

Atmosphere of Suspense

The writer of the Book of Ruth is painting graphic word pictures for his readers. It does no injustice to Scripture if we believe that those who first listened to the story, or had it read to them, were hoping that Boaz and Ruth would eventually marry. Now all seems lost. Those who are anticipating a happy ending to the story have heard the unnamed kinsman say, "I will redeem the land." They know that Ruth is bound up in this transaction. They fear that the "villain" may go off with the "heroine" after all.

Boaz has acted with integrity in giving his relative the right of first refusal. Will his honesty result in his personal loss?

Boaz still has something to relate to his kinsman. He says in effect, "On the day that you buy the field from the hand of Naomi, you must also take the hand of Ruth [in marriage] and raise up the name of the dead on his plot of ground" (4:5).

Fall of the Domino

With a remarkably rapid change of heart, Elimelech's relative says, "I cannot redeem it for myself, lest I jeopardize my own inheritance. Redeem it for yourself. You take my right of redemption, for I cannot redeem it" (4:6).

Why this sudden change in attitude? The German evangelical Bible scholars, Friedrick Keil and Franz Delitzsch, explained the would-be redeemer's changed motivation:

> If he [had] acquired the field by redemption as his own permanent property, he would have increased by so much his own possessions in land. But if he should marry Ruth, the field so redeemed would belong to the son whom he would beget through her, and he would therefore have parted with the money that he had paid for the redemption merely for the son of Ruth, so that he would have withdrawn a certain amount of capital from his own possession, and to that extent have detracted from its worth.[29]

Flawed Heritage

Ironically, this Bethlehemite who was so concerned about preserving his heritage, has been forgotten. Samuel Cox stated:

> It is a curious comment on his narrow, selfish ambition that, of this man who was bent on preserving his name and fame, who would run no risk of having his name cut from his place, neither Israel nor the world even so much as remembers [his] mere name. He is unnamed in the very Book which recounts his story; we know him simply as the "anonymous kinsman"; while Boaz, who had no such selfish ambition, who held that in every nation they who trust God and work righteousness are acceptable with Him, lives on forever on the sacred page,

and is enrolled, together with Ruth, in the pedigree of Him whose Name is above every name.[30]

The facelessness of Elimelech's kinsman reminds me of something I once read about a famous painting by John Singer Sargent (1856–1925). He was approached by Miss Elizabeth Garrett, the founder of Johns Hopkins Medical School, to paint a group portrait of the four men who had brought such renown to the institution: Drs. Welch, Halstead, Osler, and Kelly.

From the very beginning, Dr. Welch did not get along with Sargent. He complained that Sargent called them all "Kelly" and objected to the way they were to pose. He so angered John Sargent that he was told he would be painted so that his facial features would gradually fade and he would not be remembered by posterity.

The painting of "The Four Doctors" still hangs (I am told) in the Medical School of Johns Hopkins University, but the face of Dr. William Henry Welch is steadily fading. Those who walk the halls of this prestigious university can no longer discern what Dr. Welch looked like.

Those who give of themselves in the service of others are remembered, as Boaz is to this day, for those qualities of character that truly made them great.

SINGLED OUT

Boaz's dealings with the kinsman illustrate, as Richard Watson has pointed out, that "a good man will have everything done with perfect openness and honor and will stand by the result whether it meets his hopes or disappoints them."[31]

Righteous over Much?

We cannot help but notice the integrity of the one whom Naomi has singled out as the best prospective husband for Ruth. Boaz was frank in his approach and straightforward in his business dealings. He was also aware of the social custom of his people. At no time did he give offense, either by word or deed. His relative had the prior claim to redeem Naomi's land, and he not only advised him of his right but also recommended that he exercise it. All his actions were characterized by a sense of justness too little found among God's people today.

RUTH 3:14–4:6

The Matter of Discernment

Boaz was also discreet. In our day he illustrates the kind of person who will put important things in writing. In his day he obtains ten reliable witnesses to attest to what took place. He does not select people of inferior standing in the community whose word might be altered with a suitable bribe. Instead, he chooses reliable people whose trustworthiness and knowledge were well established. These he summons to witness all that transpires.

The Mix-up over Emotions

No doubt Boaz wished personally to marry Ruth. She appealed to him. The qualities of her character matched his own. He, therefore, faced a tension between his personal desires and his familial duty. How was this tension to be resolved? Certainly not by ignoring the rights of others or having a clandestine relationship. The tension was resolved by doing the right thing in the right way.

Boaz's integrity kept his task in perspective and his desires in their place. As a result, his emotions did not obstruct his reason. He could make the basic issues known to his kinsman; and then because he was able to control the pace as well as the content of the meeting, he could advise his relative of a responsibility that accompanied the purchase of the land, namely, marriage to Ruth.

What Experience Tells Us

The kind of practical righteousness Boaz demonstrated is not often found in Christian circles. We often lack patience, are selfish, and play "political games" in order to get what we want. Our thoughts and desires are centered on ourselves. We find it easy to excuse our actions. We blame our hang-ups on our parents, our materialism on the economy, and our inordinate desire for certain things on social trends, and we secretly excuse our conduct by comparing ourselves with other people. We conclude, "Well, I'm not so bad after all."

Only as we open our hearts to the searching light of Holy Scripture and compare our conduct with what is revealed in God's Word do we realize how mercenary, self-centered, and ungodly we may have become.

What then are we to do if we would be characterized by the kind of practical righteousness illustrated by a man such as Boaz?

RUTH 3:14–4:6

The answer may be found in Boaz's Godward orientation. He lived out his life—faced the effects of a lengthy famine, achieved a reputation for his ability to lead Bethlehem's band of militia, had a positive influence on his workers, took the initiative when necessary, and conducted himself honorably in a variety of circumstances—conscious all the while that God's eye was on him. It was no wonder that in crucial situations the uprightness of his character shined as clearly as the sun's rays on the shimmering waters of a lake.

We too may exhibit the same moral probity and practical maturity if we remember that the bricks of character are laid one by one. In the same way that character takes time to develop, so does the kind of maturity and instinctively right conduct found in a person such as Boaz.

The place to begin is with a renewed commitment of one's entire life to the Lord. With this foundation, we can build a consistent pattern of doing the right thing in the right way. Self-restraint and, on occasion, self-sacrifice will be needed. To this will be added the importance of fulfilling one's moral duties (as Boaz did), along with the ability to speak the truth in love to one's neighbor.

The more we ponder Ruth 4 and internalize its message, the greater will be our growth toward spiritual maturity.

RUTH 3:14–4:6

ך HOW WE
8 SHOULD LIVE

Ruth
4:7–13

One evidence of spiritual maturity is graciousness.

Inevitably people become like the thing or things they worship. This was true of people living in Old Testament times, and it is true of us today. Human nature has not changed. It remains the same. The things we covet (i.e., wealth, success, popularity, influence, possessions of one sort or another) are spoken of in the New Testament as "idols" (cf. Col. 3:5) that we worship. They come between us and God. An eclipse takes place—one that may last for many years or even a lifetime.

Robert Wilder dramatized the effect of worshiping "other gods" in his seedy portrayal of the lust for power and wealth, *Flamingo Road*.[1] The characters are aptly drawn. Each is protrayed as intent on increasing his or her standing in the community by whatever means possible. Often this is accomplished at the expense of others. Only on rare occasions does one glimpse real concern for the downtrodden and exploited. Instead, a picture of immorality is painted in which people are treated as things, and things as if they were people.

By way of contrast, the more we are taken up with God and his goodness,[2] the more we take on his likeness (cf. 2 Cor. 3:18). One of the characteristics of such growth is graciousness. God is a God of grace (cf. Exod. 19:4; 20:6; Deut. 7:7ff.). He delights in demonstrating his loving-kindness to those who are the recipients of his grace.

The doctrine of grace is fleshed out in the New Testament. The Lord Jesus Christ is the personification of the grace of God (John 1:17), the express image of his person (Heb. 1:3).

Whether in the Old Testament or the New, God is seen dealing graciously with his people. And as he is, so we should be in the world.

In our study of the Book of Ruth, we have already come across the word *hesed*. The term describes God's steadfast love. The Hebrew scholar of a generation past, Dr. William Gesenius, believed that *hesed* characterized an "eager and ardent desire by which anyone is led."[3]

In the Old Testament, *hesed* was frequently translated "loving-kindness." It involved a relationship on the basis of which acts of kindness are performed. Such relationships can exist between peers (e.g., David and Jonathan), a king and his subjects (e.g., David and the people of Israel), God and a nation, or God and an individual.

The basis of God's relationships has always been his firm, persistent, and steadfast love. This does not mean that he cannot or will not chasten those whom he loves (Heb. 12:8–11). It does mean that when chastening becomes necessary, it is carried out with our good as the goal. Our response to God's grace should be twofold: (1) We should respond to him in loving obedience to his will, and (2) we should demonstrate the same kind of *hesed* in our relationships with others. This, as we have seen, was the basis of Naomi's home in Moab (1:8), and it does not surprise us that Orpah and Ruth loved her.

In the New Testament, the word used to describe this attitude of God toward us is *charis*, "grace." It is one of the great words of our Christian vocabulary. *Charis* is related to the word *chara*, "joy." Grace really means "that which causes joy." Only in the presence of the Lord is there fullness of joy (Ps. 16:11), and so salvation—which is by grace and quite apart from works (Eph. 2:8–9)—is the act of God whereby, on account of his love for us, he takes us out of the helpless state in which sin holds us captive, releases us, and restores us to a right standing before him. All this is done by God and is based solely on the sacrificial death of Christ on our behalf. This new experience of grace is designed to make possible our experience of "fullness of joy."[4]

RUTH 4:7–13

MANIFESTATIONS OF GRACE

Following the near-kinsman's refusal to redeem both Ruth *and* the land (4:6), the writer provided an explanation of what took place at the gate of the city. The Book of Deuteronomy stated:

If the kinsman does not desire to take his brother's wife, then his brother's wife shall go up to the gate to the elders and say, "My husband's brother refuses to establish a name for his brother in Israel; he is not willing to perform the duty of a kinsman to me." . . . Then his brother's wife shall come to him in the sight of the elders, and pull his sandal off his foot and spit in his face. . . . And in Israel his name shall be called, "The house of him whose sandal is removed" (25:7–10).

The writer of Ruth explains:

And this [was] formerly [done][5] in Israel concerning redemption, and concerning the exchange [of property], to confirm[6] every matter: a man would draw off[7] his sandal and give [it] to his neighbor; and this was the attestation[8] in Israel. And the kinsman said to Boaz, "You acquire for yourself." And he[9] drew off his sandal (4:7–8).

In these verses from Ruth, we notice two important aspects of grace: (1) the gracious maturity of the writer and (2) the kindness of the elders.

The writer is steadily developing our interest in Boaz and Ruth. They are noble in character, mature in their personhood, and in every way commend themselves to those who admire the best in other people. It would be easy for the writer to speak contemptuously or scornfully of anyone opposing Boaz or Ruth or doing them any harm.

When Elimelech's relative refuses to redeem the poverty-stricken widows, we might have expected some evidence of the writer's disdain. Scripture had already established a precedent that such a person be exposed to public shame and referred to by the unflattering name of "Baresole." The narrator, however, treats the relative of Elimelech with gentleness. He continues to refer to the kinsman as *gō'ēl* "redeemer" (4:8).

The elders are also gracious. They permit the unnamed kinsman to take off his shoe and give it to Boaz without summoning Ruth to their meeting and having her humiliate him before the residents of the city.

RUTH 4:7–13

Was such an act as theirs one of weakness? Did they tolerate the
flouting of God's law because they lacked the conviction to uphold
it? Were they guilty of improper compromise? It would appear that
they were not. In the presence of righteousness, the conduct of the
unrighteous is exposed. Before men of integrity, a person whose
actions are prompted by ulterior motives stands rebuked. His
shame, therefore, arises from within himself. His own heart con-
demns him. Only where righteousness is not practiced consistently
by those in positions of responsibility is it necessary to insist on
"the letter of the law."

Significant Gesture

Elimelech's unnamed kinsman does not lack for critics. Hardly
any commentator has spoken well of him. Next to Boaz, the imper-
fections of his character stand out clearly. Note the gracelessness of
his reply to Boaz in 4:8. The Hebrew conveys the terseness of his
response: "Buy for yourself."

"Buy what?" we may ask. Is Ruth so contemptible a creature that
she is unworthy of a name? Is such disdain for a human being
justifiable? Why should a person who has a few moments ago responded with alacrity by saying, "I will buy Naomi's plot of ground,"
now respond in such an abrasive manner?

The answer to this kinsman's gracelessness seems to lie in the
fact that he feels himself caught on the horns of a dilemma. And
there are plenty of people present to witness his discomfort. He is
trapped by his own greed. When he learns from Boaz that Naomi is
compelled to sell her land, and knowing that she has no heirs to
reclaim it from him, he readily agrees to perform the duty of a *gō'ēl*
according to the law of Moses (Lev. 25:23ff.).

By assuming the responsibilities of a redeemer in one area (i.e.,
the "redemption" of the land Naomi is selling), he places himself
under all legislation applying to a kinsman—one of the functions of
that concerned "brother-in-law (levirate) marriage." When Boaz
mentions the need to marry Ruth (4:5), the kinsman quickly backs
off.[10] No economic advantage is to be gained by marrying Ruth. The
kinsman senses inwardly how his own emotions have betrayed him
and so says tersely to Boaz, "Buy for yourself."

William Taylor summed up his attitude: "One thing . . . is very
clear, namely that his whole thought was about his own inheritance,
and thus selfishness was at the root of his decision."[11]

RUTH 4:7-13

Ruth is not present at the gate and the elders of the city do not summon her. The kinsman, to avoid further public humiliation, voluntarily removes his sandal and gives it to Boaz. In doing so, he transfers to Boaz his right to act as the *gō'ēl* of Ruth and Naomi.

The significance of this act has been described by James Morison. "He who sold land, or surrendered his right to act as a kinsman in buying land, intimated by the symbolic act of taking off his shoe, and handing it to his friend, that he freely gave up his right to walk on the soil, in favor of the person who had acquired possession."[12]

LETTER OF THE LAW

With the right to act as Naomi's and Ruth's redeemer now legally assigned to him, Boaz turns to the elders and all the people, and says:

[You are] witnesses[13] today that I have acquired all that [belonged] to Elimelech, and all that [belonged] to Chilion and Mahlon,[14] from the hand of Naomi; and also Ruth the Moabitess,[15] the wife of Mahlon, I have acquired for myself to be my wife, to raise up the name of the dead on his inheritance, so that the name of the dead shall not be cut off from among his brothers, or from the gate of his people [lit., place];[16] you are witnesses today (4:9–10).

The morning's events have been very taxing for Boaz. He has consistently done what is right, regardless of his personal preferences. Now, in a carefully worded legal statement, he outlines all that he proposes to do for Elimelech's widow and daughter-in-law.

Boaz's emotion is evident in his words, yet his feelings remain under control. His graciousness may be seen in his refraining from drawing any unpleasant contrast between his conduct and that of Elimelech's near kinsman. Instead, Boaz carefully outlines all that he is acquiring and clearly states his intention to take Ruth as his wife. He does not forget his obligations and affirms before all present that their first son will inherit Mahlon's estate and perpetuate his name.

More than Good Intentions

Boaz's activity at the village gate illustrates the principle of grace. George Knight has reminded us that if a mere man, a creature of God, could behave in the manner described, and had indeed by his action exhibited the power to redeem an outcast and bring her into fellowship with the living God, then two things could be said of the Creator of Boaz—(1) God must feel at least as compassionate towards all the Ruths of Moab and of Babylon and of every other land as his creature Boaz felt towards Ruth; (2) God must actually be a God of redemption, with the desire and the power to redeem all outcasts into fellowship with himself.[17]

Bridging the Gap

Many Bible scholars have seen in Boaz's role as a *kinsman-redeemer* a parallel with the Lord Jesus Christ.

First, according to Leviticus 25:23ff. and Deuteronomy 25:7–10, the redeemer must be a near relative. When this truth is compared to the teaching of the New Testament, the necessity for Christ's incarnation becomes clear. He needed to share our humanity (cf. Heb. 2:14), and so he became our Kinsman "according to the flesh" in order that he might redeem us from sin.

Second, a kinsman in Israel could not exercise the right of redemption if he himself were in debt, had sold part of his own estate, or were too poor to do so. This brings into focus the reason for the temptation of Jesus Christ. Through his temptation he demonstrated that his "estate" (i.e., his person) had not been mortgaged to sin. He was free from both a sin nature and sinful practices (Heb. 4:15). He could say to his disciples, "The prince of this world comes and has no power over me" (John 14:30). Christ was therefore able to perform the part of our Kinsman and redeem us from our bankrupt state.

Lastly, Boaz illustrated the fact that the kinsman must be willing to pay the price and buy back the mortgaged inheritance of another. This could only be done at high personal cost. In the case of the Lord Jesus, he willingly went to the cross to accomplish our redemption (John 10:15b, 18a; 1 Pet. 3:18).

The story of Boaz illuminates the New Testament doctrine of redemption. To understand this doctrine, we must picture a slave market where people are enslaved by sin (Rom. 7:14). From this position Christ buys us and then releases us. Sin, however, has been committed, and sin is always viewed as being committed against God. The ransom must therefore be paid to him. Christ paid the price for our redemption. God has declared himself satisfied (1 John

2:2), and on the basis of Christ's work for us, he can now deal with us in grace. And we in gratitude can render him loving service.

TIMELY BENEDICTION

Boaz's willingness to redeem Naomi and marry Ruth evokes the praise of all who have witnessed the proceedings. They give a spontaneous expression of their admiration in the form of a benediction.[18]

> May *Yahweh* grant that the woman who has come[19] into your house [be] as Rachel and as Leah,[20] both of whom[21] built the house of Israel; and may you achieve wealth [lit., act worthily][22] in Ephrathah and become famous [lit., {be} called a name][23] in Bethlehem. And may your house be like the house of Perez whom Tamar bore to Judah, through the seed which *Yahweh* shall give you of this young woman[24] (4:11–12).

The people and the elders respond to Boaz by affirming their status as witnesses and by pronouncing a blessing on him and Ruth.

Misplaced Priorities

It is hard to imagine a more uncomfortable position than the one occupied by Elimelech's unnamed near-kinsman. To be desirous of those things that would enhance his own prestige and reputation, and then to hear the elders bestowing their accolades on Boaz, as well as wishing him prosperity and fame, must have caused him considerable personal discomfort, if not outright envy.

He reminds us of those whose thoughts and actions are controlled by worldly considerations. They may prosper for a time, but they are seldom satisfied. Their possessions are never quite sufficient; their crops are never quite as good as they had hoped; their work never quite earns for them the recognition they believe they deserve; and as they grow older, their thoughts are frequently dominated by what might have been.

How much better to live as Boaz did, do what is right, and enjoy the blessing of God on one's life.

The Invocation of Blessing

A unique characteristic of Judaism and Christianity is that their adherents possess the power to bless. In pagan religions power is derived from the ability to punish or curse.[25] The word *bārak* "to bless," in the Old Testament was used as a form of a benediction (cf. Num. 6:23–27), an act of worship (Ps. 103), or a transmittal of something from someone who is greater to someone of lesser status or ability (Heb. 7:7).

The term "to bless" (*bārak*) is closely related to the word for "knee" (*berek*). Some believed this connection derived from "bowing the knee" in acknowledgment of God's past favors (Gen. 24:26; Deut. 8:10). The Old Testament sees the verb "to bless" and its derivatives "blessing" and "blessedness" as having God as the source. The blessings of his covenant extend to every area of life (Deut. 28:3–6) and are attributable to his gracious character (cf. Deut. 23:5).[26]

Because God's rule over his creation was through people whom he had chosen, he had delegated to his representatives the power to pronounce blessing in his name.[27] This was why Isaac's blessing of Jacob and Esau (Gen. 27), or Jacob's blessing of his sons (Gen. 48–49) became, in a sense, a prophecy of them and their descendants. This was also why Eli could promise Hannah that her prayer would be answered (1 Sam. 1:9–18, 20).

As responsibility for acting on God's behalf was diversified, the ability to bless people in the name of the Lord (i.e., as if God were present) was shared among different kinds of leaders (cf. Num. 11:16–25). Because this gift came more and more to be identified with the Holy Spirit, the indwelling and filling by the Spirit of God places us in a position to be a blessing to, and confer blessing on, other people. That blessing is a gracious activity of God on our behalf whereby he enriches our lives by supplying us with that which we lack.

Days of Austerity?

In the blessing of the elders of the city and the general benediction of the people, they pray that the Lord will grant Boaz prosperity. Boaz was probably not a wealthy man, although we do not know for sure. His financial resources may have been severely depleted during the years of famine (as had everyone else's); and possibly he already had a wife and family, for polygamy was permitted under Mosaic law (cf. Deut. 21:15ff). In light of these likely circumstances, we see why the people of Bethlehem desire that he "act

RUTH 4:7–13

worthily [i.e., become prosperous] in Ephratah and become famous in Bethlehem."[28]

TOGETHER AT LAST

With the blessing of the people of Bethlehem still sounding in his ears, Boaz makes his way to the humble cottage of Naomi. From what transpires later on (4:16), we conclude that Boaz took both women to his home.

We do not know what kind of reception Naomi and Ruth receive from the other members of Boaz's household. They only learn of Ruth's nocturnal claim on Boaz when he returns from the threshing floor shortly before dawn. Adjustments are never easy to make, particularly when these mean a change in one's life-style. We can only hope that Boaz's household acted as graciously toward Ruth and Naomi as Boaz, the elders, and the people had done.

The biblical text merely states:

> And Boaz took Ruth, and she became his wife, and he went in to her;[29] and *Yahweh* gave her conception [i.e., enabled her to conceive], and she gave birth to a son (4:13).

Ruth has not had much time to prepare herself mentally or emotionally for marriage to Boaz. But experience does not provide an excuse for young people to rush into marriage. The old axiom "Marry in haste, repent at leisure" needs no further ratification.

Ruth's marriage to Boaz does illustrate the importance of *being* the right mate rather than trying to find the right mate. Of course, she would have to make adjustments in the household of Boaz, but we may be sure that she brings to the situation the same maturity and graciousness that characterize her throughout the story.

A number of people were involved in bringing about the eventual marriage of Ruth but God did the most of all. A short time before, Naomi had despaired of her daughter-in-law finding "rest" among her people. She had recommended that each daughter-in-law return to her mother's home and seek a husband among her own people (1:8–9, 11–16). That which seemed utterly impossible to achieve from a human standpoint, God in his infinite wisdom and steadfast love accomplished for Ruth in the land in which she was an alien.

As Leon Morris pointed out, "the son that was born is regarded as God's gift."[30] He then reminded us that "throughout this book there is the consistent thought that God is over all and works out his will. We have seen that the elders and others regarded children as God's gift (4:12), and we see the same thought now from the author."[31] Ruth, though childless in her first marriage, was now able to bear a son. Such an occurrence must surely have been evidence of his blessing.[32]

THE SOURCE

Considering the numerous illustrations of God's providential care and provision found throughout the Book of Ruth, we are led sooner or later to search for their underlying cause. Did he single out Ruth and graciously elect her to be the recipient of his favor while denying the same blessings to others?

This question is more than academic. Its answer spells the difference between hope and disillusionment for each of us. The writer has shown us repeatedly that a definite relationship exists between fidelity and its reward. He has emphasized Ruth's piety, her loyalty to Naomi (1:8; 2:11; 3:10), which involved obedience to the revealed will of God, her diligence in caring for Naomi (2:2, 7), and her moral integrity.

The blessings of God were the result of a relationship. The name for God used most frequently throughout this book is *Yahweh*. This is only one of the many names for God, but it was specifically used of him in relation to his covenant with the people of Israel.

When the emphasis on relationship (stressed repeatedly by the use of the name *Yahweh*) is coupled with the practice of obedience, we have the key elements to the secret of spiritual growth and the enjoyment of God's blessings. He desires a relationship with us. He has demonstrated his loving-kindness and steadfast desire for what is best for us. If our response to him is positive and characterized by obedience, then we too may enjoy the evidences of his blessing, which we see abundantly illustrated for us in this brief story.

In reflecting on these incidents, Dr. William M. Taylor said, "Not every story that begins so sadly as this did has so sweet and pleasant an ending. Not always are virtue, piety, constancy, and self-sacrifice so visibly rewarded on the earth. But we are not on that account to think less of the providence of God; for virtue is not to be pursued because of its reward, and right is to be done for its own sake—nay, rather, for the sake of God. Then, when the end shall come . . . we shall see the vindication of Jehovah."[33]

RUTH 4:7–13

7 9 NAOMI'S RECOMPENSE

Ruth
4:14–22

The name of John Calvin is revered by students of Scripture all over the world. Whether we agree with all that he wrote or not, the fact is that theologians quote extensively from his *Institutes of the Christian Religion,* and sociologists study his system of ethics. Politicians analyze the impact of his principles on democracy, and historians evaluate the effect of his influence on succeeding generations. It has become popular in our day to publish biographies about him, issue new translations of his works, and compile bibliographies listing works about him.

Few of us who laud the great accomplishments of "the genius of Geneva"[1] recall that he was not always held in such high esteem. To show their contempt for him, some of the people of Geneva called their dogs "Calvin." Then, when they saw him passing by, they would call "Calvin, Calvin"; and as he turned in their direction, they would stoop down and pet their dogs.

On one occasion, when the libertine faction in Geneva became powerful, they rallied their forces against those who stood for truth and righteousness and banished John Calvin from their city. The great reformer's reaction to the bitterness and hatred of his enemies has been preserved for us by his biographers: "Most assuredly if I had merely served man, this would have been poor recompense; but it is my happiness that I have served Him who never fails to reward His servants to the full extent of His promise."[2]

Calvin's words "who never fails to *reward* His servants to the full extent of His promise" describe Ruth's experience and our confidence in him.

THE PRINCIPLE OF REWARD

"Reward" differs from "payment" as the apostle Paul makes clear in Romans 4:4. We are remunerated for our services, but to receive a reward is entirely dependent on someone else's kindness toward us. A reward is the result of grace.

The Bible teaches us that there are degrees of reward depending on our faithfulness to God's revealed will. Furthermore, the Lord Jesus often used the promise of future recompense as an incentive to loyal service. And the writer of Hebrews explained that Moses chose to endure ill-treatment with the people of God, rather than enjoy the passing pleasures of sin; *for he was looking to the reward* (Heb. 11:24–26)—God's eternal recompense of his devotion.

The full extent of God's gracious goodwill toward us is hard to imagine. The apostle Paul admitted his inability to describe it when he wrote, "Things which eye has not seen and ear has not heard, and which have not entered the heart of man, all that God has prepared for those who love him" (1 Cor. 2:9).

The concept of reward differed in the Old Testament from the teaching of the New, and yet they were connected. In the Old Testament, the blessing of God was both material and spiritual. The condition to be met was a simple one, namely, obedience to his covenant.[3] When this requirement had been met, a threefold blessing would result: (1) continuance as a nation in the land; (2) blessing from God in all areas of life; and (3) anticipation of the fullness of blessing under the reign of the Messiah.

When the Lord Jesus came he offered himself to the nation as their long-awaited Messiah. Unfortunately for Israel, they rejected him (cf. Matt. 11:2–12:50). All the material blessings of his Kingdom reign have had to be postponed.[4] We now live in the *interim* between his two advents.[5] Blessings still accrue to those who obey his revealed will. The emphasis now is on a *future* reward rather than temporal prosperity (cf. 1 Cor. 9:25; James 1:12; Rev. 2:10).

The German evangelical Bible scholar Dr. Bernard Weiss grasped the essence of this truth when he wrote:

As the servants of God in the Israelitish theocracy[6] were entitled, by reason of their covenant relationship, to look for the fulfillment of the promise as the reward for their fulfillment of their covenant obligations, so the disciple of Jesus is entitled to look for the completion of salvation [i.e., his glorification and being forever with the Lord] as the

RUTH 4:14–22

reward for the fulfillment of the demands which are made on him in virtue of his being a disciple.[7]

Naomi and God's recompense to her are central in the closing section of the Book of Ruth. One important principle found here is that *God graciously rewards those who faithfully follow him and are obedient to his Word.*

A BRIGHTER FUTURE

Boaz and Ruth have both appeared on the stage for the last time. They now enjoy one of those rare unions in which both husband and wife[8] are selfless and mature, empathetic and understanding, united in their values and goals, and therefore able to grow together personally and spiritually.

As the story began with Naomi, so now it ends with her. The women of the city who shunned her after her return from Moab now gather around her and are profuse in their praise. They see evidence of God's favor toward her and feel that they can now show their approval.

> "Blessed [be] *Yahweh*, who has not left you without [lit., caused to fail] a near kinsman;[9] and may his name[10] be called in Israel [i.e., may he become famous]. And may he become to you a restorer of life[11] and a nourisher of your old age; for your daughter-in-law, who loves you,[12] and is better to you than seven sons,[13] has borne him."
>
> And Naomi took the child and laid him in her bosom,[14] and became his nurse.
>
> And the neighborhood women[15] gave him a name, saying, "A son has been born to Naomi"; and they called his name Obed. He is the father of Jesse, the father of David (4:14–17).

Change of Fortune

Samuel Cox provided a final connection between the preceding scene and what we find recorded in these verses.

> Boaz, being now the recognized *goel* of Ruth, marries her; and in due time a son is given to them. And now the shadows, which lay so thick on the opening incidents of the Story, clear off, and both Naomi and Ruth receive a full reward for their rare and heroic love. It is one of the many fine points of the Story that its concluding sentences are

almost wholly devoted, not to the young and happy wife and mother, but to Naomi, who had suffered so many calamities, and who, by the piety and resignation with which she bore them, had drawn Ruth from the idolatries of Moab. It is Naomi, not Ruth, whom "the women her neighbors" congratulate on the birth of Ruth's son. In him they see Naomi's *goel*—Ruth already had hers in Boaz; and they pray that, as he grows up, he may restore her to her former happiness and be the stay and gladness of her old age. But though they speak to Naomi, and pray for her, they do not utterly forget the singular virtue of Ruth. In the words, "thy daughter-in-law, *who loveth thee, who is better to thee than seven sons,*" they pronounce on her an eulogy such as few "strange" women could have heard from Hebrew lips. It is because the boy is Ruth's son that he is Naomi's *goel;* for how can he fail to love and cherish the woman whom his mother has loved with a love even passing that of women?[16]

God has blessed Naomi. He has brought the impossible to pass (cf. 1:11–12 with 4:17). She had gone to Moab of her own accord and, following the death of Elimelech, had stayed there of her own free will. Her sons had died in that land, and she had been left with her grief.

With the passing of her loved ones, Naomi doubtless felt acute anxiety, for she had been left alone in the world. She may also have felt anger because of the bitterness in her heart toward God and the helplessness of her situation (cf. 1:20–21). And she may also have felt some guilt, for she acknowledged that "the hand of *Yahweh*" had gone out against her (i.e., to chasten her).

Naomi, however, had turned her back on Moab and returned to the place of God's appointment. As one who had repented of a former wrong, she had cast herself on him and his mercy. Her welcome back to Bethlehem left much to be desired. Her former friends, following their initial greeting, left her strictly alone. "The Lord," they concluded, "is obviously displeased with her; and, as evidence of his continued displeasure, a Moabitess accompanies her. The marriages of her sons to foreigners had obviously been the cause of their deaths." And so Naomi was left on her own to cope as best she could.

But Naomi's fortune has changed, and now these same women speak glowingly of God's goodness to her. Ruth's newborn son is regarded as Naomi's *gō'ēl*, or "redeemer." Certainly Boaz continues in the role of Naomi's supporter, but Obed, who is looked on as

RUTH 4:14–22

Mahlon's child (cf. 4:10), is to be to her a "restorer of life and a nourisher of her old age."

So it is that God shows special kindness to Naomi. When her sons died in Moab, she had nothing to live for. Hope was gone. Now in honoring her faithfulness to his covenant, he has given her a (grand) son. Ruth's child is her reward.

Unnoticed No Longer

Ruth also receives the praise of the women of the village. On their return from Moab, Ruth had gone unnoticed. The women came out to greet Naomi, but Ruth was not made welcome. Now they say to Naomi that *Yahweh* has more than compensated her for the loss of Mahlon and Chilion (4:15*b*). Ruth is better than seven sons.

Leon Morris commented on their words:

> The love of Ruth for her mother-in-law shines through this book and it is appropriate that it be given this recognition at the end. The tribute, *which is better to thee than seven sons* (AV, RV; *cf.* I Sa. 1:8), is all the more striking in view of the place usually given boys in comparison with girls. A numerous male progeny was the ambition of all married people and thus to speak of Ruth as being worth more to Naomi than *seven sons* is the supreme tribute. For *seven sons* is proverbial for a perfect family, *cf.* I Samuel 2:5.[17]

Forgotten now is Ruth's Moabitish ancestry; forgotten too are her years of barrenness, which those who were superstitious may have felt was a punishment from God for some previous sin. Ruth has borne Naomi a son in accordance with the principles of God's covenant. She now receives belated but deserved praise.

Rite of Spring

With renewed hope in her heart, Naomi takes Ruth's son to her heart and showers on him all the love and devotion of a grateful grandmother. She had despaired of ever having grandchildren, and now what was thought to be impossible, God has graciously brought to pass.

We can understand some of Naomi's gladness when we consider that "to Naomi this child was special. She had expected a lonely old age when her husband and sons died. With none of those near to her left her future had indeed looked bleak. But thanks to Ruth's devotion everything was now different. She belonged to a family once more. She was loved and she had a recognized place. The babe in a sense symbolized it all, and Naomi gave herself over to caring for him."[18]

What's in a Name?

The neighbors of Boaz also come and rejoice with Naomi. These women gather about Naomi and give the young child the name Obed (meaning "servant").

We are surprised that Boaz does not give a name to his own son. The closest parallel to this incident in Ruth 4 is to be found in Luke 1. There, at the birth of the son of Zacharias and Elizabeth, their neighbors and relatives gathered in the home and suggested that the child be named after his father. Only after the protests of his parents was he named John.

Perhaps because Naomi had no living relatives and because the child was legally reckoned as the son of Mahlon, the women gather around her and suggest the name Obed. The idea of the lad growing up to serve his grandmother must have struck a responsive chord in their hearts, and so he is called "Servant"—Naomi's helper, the mainstay of her old age.

Further evidence of God's goodness to Naomi may be found in the fact that, in time, Obed himself will marry. Naomi's great-grandson will be called Jesse, and his (and her great-great-grandson) will be named David. And in time David will become Israel's great king.

Through these descendants and the loving care of Ruth and Boaz, God amply rewards Naomi and fully meets all her needs.

LINKED WITH ROYALTY

The mention of Naomi's connection with David prompted the writer to conclude with a genealogy. The importance of these lists of names to Israelites has been underscored by Dr. Marshall D. Johnson in his book *The Purpose of the Biblical Genealogies.* He points out that these genealogies were designed "to establish continuity over those periods of time not covered by material in the tradition."

Having laid down this general principle, Johnson observes that "The *Tōlēdôth* (i.e., genealogy) of Perez appended to the book of

Ruth (4:18–22) may similarly be intended to establish continuity during the time of the judges, that is, from the conquest [of the land by Joshua] to the beginning of the Davidic monarch."[19]

There are some important things to notice in the genealogy, in particular its beginning with Perez the son of Tamar (Gen. 38; Matt. 1:3).

> And these [are] the generations of Perez: Perez fathered Hezron, and Hezron fathered Ram, and Ram fathered Amminadab, and Amminadab fathered Nashon, and Nashon fathered Salmon, and Salmon fathered Boaz, and Boaz fathered Obed, and Obed fathered Jesse, and Jesse fathered David (4:18–22).

The Recompense of Reward

This genealogy at the end of the Book of Ruth was probably incomplete. The famous Hebraists, Keil and Delitzsch, pointed out that Perez's son Hezron was born *before* Jacob went down to Egypt (cf. Gen. 38:29 and 46:12). This took place around 1875 B.C. The Exodus from Egypt occurred around 1445 B.C., leaving more than 430 years to be covered from Perez to Nashon. "According to this there are only four or five generations to the 430 years spent by the Israelites in Egypt."[20]

Keil and Delitzsch continued: "The omission of the unimportant members becomes still more apparent in the statement that follows, *vis.,* that Nashon begat *Salmah* [Salmon], and Salmah, *Boaz*, in which only two generations are given for a space of more than 250 years."[21]

Such facts should not disturb us, for it is evident from other genealogies that the lists in the Bible are representative.[22]

Not only was the genealogy incomplete but also Boaz's name appeared. Obed was regarded as the son of Mahlon, not Boaz; therefore the mention of Boaz is somewhat surprising.

It seems as if the blessing of the elders and the people at the city gate (see 4:11*b*–12) was borne out in the history of events, when they said to Boaz:

> May you prosper in Ephrathah and be renowned in Bethlehem; and may your house be like the house of Perez, whom Tamar bore to Judah, because of the children whom *Yahweh* shall give you by this young woman.

RUTH 4:14–22

Mahlon seems to have been bypassed in David's ancestral record in favor of Boaz.

Morris commented that "Obed [in this genealogy] is treated simply as the son of Boaz. In a sense he carried on Mahlon's name and succeeded to his property. But in an official genealogy he is treated as the son of his true father."[23]

However true this might be, may we not be overlooking God's gracious recompense of *Boaz* by linking him with David? It seems preferable to include the idea that the writer, under the gentle leading of the Holy Spirit, had artlessly shown God's favor to Boaz as well as Naomi.

A final observation about the genealogy concerns Ruth. Her name appeared in the genealogy of the Lord Jesus Christ (Matt. 1:5). There she was linked with Tamar and Rahab. This was most unusual, for women were not normally included in such records. C. H. Spurgeon, the famous British expositor of the nineteenth century, in tracing the ancestral line of the Lord Jesus, commented on the inclusion of Ruth in his genealogy. "We note that . . . Gentile blood mingled with the Hebrew strain. Our King [Christ] . . . is heir of a line in which flows the blood of . . . the rustic *Ruth*; he is akin to the fallen and the lowly, and he will show his love even to the poorest and the most obscure."[24] In his birth, the Lord Jesus demonstrated his grace toward us by being identified with our humanity.

More than an Appendix

But some will ask, why did the writer end his story so abruptly? Why did he conclude with a list of names? Wasn't this a strange way to finish a book? What did God intend us to learn from these verses?

The author did not tell us why he finished his book this way. The concluding paragraphs emphasized God's grace to Ruth in her marriage to Boaz and his favor toward Naomi. It seems, therefore, as if the verses that ended this story should in some way continue this theme.

By looking back at Perez and forward to David, we see how God's loving-kindness to Boaz and Ruth far exceeded their ability to imagine. He made them part of a line that led up to the great King David,[25] "a man after the heart of God" (Acts 13:22), and forever enshrined their names in the ancestry of him who is King of kings and Lord of lords.

RUTH 4:14–22

Furthermore, the genealogy, brief as it was, became a part of another record (1 Chron. 2:3ff.) and another (Matt. 1), so that we begin to glimpse God's masterful, overarching plan for our redemption. His hand controls history; he works out his purpose in the lives of his people from one generation to the next; his plan has continuity and purpose.

We may see only a few of his ways, and our understanding of them may be obscured by limitations imposed by the Fall, but these concluding verses remind us that he is over all his works; his plan cannot be thwarted; he elects to positions of honor whomsoever he will; and, while we are subject to all the limitations of the flesh, he continues to deal with us in grace and offer us the promise of a future recompense if we will but obey him. Of his kind intent toward the lowliest of his followers, his dealings with Naomi and Ruth furnish ample proof!

RUTH 4:14–22

APPENDIXES

APPENDICES

ABBREVIATIONS

AJSL	*American Journal of Semitic Languages and Literatures*
ANET	*Ancient Near Eastern Texts*, J. B. Pritchard, ed. (Princeton, N.J.: Princeton University Press, 1969).
Archer	G. L. Archer, *Survey of Old Testament Introduction* (Chicago: Moody, 1974).
BA	*Biblical Archaeologist*
BASOR	*Bulletin of the American Society for Oriental Research*
BDB	F. Brown, S. R. Driver, and C. A. Briggs, eds., *Hebrew-English Lexicon of the Old Testament* (Oxford: Clarendon, 1907).
Bewer	J. A. Bewer, *Literature of the Old Testament* (New York: Columbia University Press, 1933).
BJRL	*Bulletin of the John Rylands Library*
BT	*Bible Translator*
Campbell	E. F. Campbell, Jr., *Ruth, A New Translation with Introduction, Notes, and Commentary*. The Anchor Bible (Garden City, N.Y.: Doubleday, 1975).
Cassell	P. Cassell, *Joshua, Judges and Ruth*. J. P. Lange's *Commentary on the Holy Scriptures* (Grand Rapids: Zondervan, n.d.).
CBQ	*Catholic Biblical Quarterly*
Cox	S. Cox, *The Book of Ruth* (London: Religious Tract Society, 1922).
deVaux	R. deVaux, *Ancient Israel*, trans. J. McHugh (New York: McGraw-Hill, 1965).
Driver	S. R. Driver, *Introduction to the Literature of the Old Testament* (Edinburgh: T. & T. Clark, 1913).
EQ	*Evangelical Quarterly*
ET	*Expository Times*
Fuerst	W. J. Fuerst, "Ruth," *Cambridge Bible Commentary* (New York: Cambridge University Press, 1975).
Fuller	T. Fuller, *A Comment on Ruth* (London: Tegg, 1868).
Gerleman	G. Gerleman, *Ruth Das Hohelied*. Biblischer Kommentar Altes Testament (Neukirchen, Switzerland: Kreis Moers, 1965).
Gray	J. Gray, *Joshua, Judges, Ruth*. New Century Bible (Grand Rapids: Eerdmans, 1967).
Harrison	R. K. Harrison, *Introduction to the Old Testament* (Grand Rapids: Eerdmans, 1969).
HDB	J. Hastings, *Dictionary of the Bible* (Edinburgh: T. & T. Clark, 1902).

Hertzberg	H. W. Hertzberg, *Die Bücher Josua, Richter, Ruth*. Das Alte Testament Deutsch (Göttingen: Vandenhoeck and Ruprecht, 1959).
HTR	*Harvard Theological Review*
IBD	J. D. Douglas, *Illustrated Bible Dictionary* (Wheaton, Ill.: Tyndale House, 1980).
JAOS	*Journal of the American Oriental Society*
JBL	*Journal of Biblical Literature*
JBR	*Journal of Bible and Religion*
JNES	*Journal of Near Eastern Studies*
Joüon, *Grammaire*	P. Joüon, *Grammaire de l'hebreu biblique* (Rome: Pontifical Biblical Institute, 1923).
Joüon, *Ruth*	P. Joüon, *Ruth, Commentaire Philologique et Exegetique* (Rome: Pontifical Biblical Institute, 1953).
JRAS	*Journal of the Royal Asiatic Society*
JTS	*Journal of Theological Studies*
KD	C. F. Keil and F. J. Delitzsch, *Biblical Commentary on the Old Testament* (Grand Rapids: Eerdmans, n.d.).
Kennedy	A. R. S. Kennedy, *The Book of Ruth* (New York: Macmillan, 1928).
Leggett	D. A. Leggett, *The Levirate and Goel Institutions in the Old Testament, with Special Reference to the Book of Ruth* (Cherry Hill, N.J.: Mack Publishing, 1974).
Morison	J. Morison, *Ruth*. The Pulpit Commentary (Grand Rapids: Eerdmans, 1963).
Morris	L. L. Morris, *Ruth*. Tyndale Old Testament Commentaries (Downers Grove, Ill.: Inter-Varsity Press, 1968).
Myers	J. M. Myers, *The Linguistic and Literary Form of the Book of Ruth* (Leiden: E. J. Brill, 1955).
PEQ	*Palestinian Exploration Quarterly*
Robinson	E. Robinson, *Biblical Researches in Palestine* (London: Murray, 1841).
Rudolph	W. Rudolph, *Das Buch Ruth, Das Hohelied, Die Klagelieder*. Kommentar zum Alten Testament (Gütersloh: J. C. Mohr, 1962).
Sasson	J. M. Sasson, *Ruth, A New Translation with a Philological Commentary and a Formalist-Folklorist Interpretation* (Baltimore: Johns Hopkins University Press, 1979).
Taylor	W. M. Taylor, *Ruth the Gleaner* (Grand Rapids: Baker, 1961 [originally published in 1886]).
TDOT	G. J. Botterweck and H. Ringgren, eds., *Theological Dictionary of the Old Testament* (Grand Rapids: Eerdmans, 1974).

TWOT	R. L. Harris, G. L. Archer, and B. K. Waltke, eds., *Theological Wordbook of the Old Testament* (Chicago: Moody, 1980).
VT	*Vetus Testamentum*
Watson	R. A. Watson, *The Book of Ruth*. The Expositor's Bible (New York: A. C. Armstrong, 1898).
Wright	C. H. H. Wright, *The Book of Ruth in Hebrew* (Leipzig: Rudolph Hartmann, 1864).
ZPEB	M. C. Tenney, ed., *Zondervan Pictorial Encyclopedia of the Bible* (Grand Rapids: Zondervan, 1975).

CRITICAL STUDIES

Important issues in the critical study of Ruth are its authorship and date, its place in the canon, and its purpose or theme.

WHO WROTE THE BOOK OF RUTH, AND WHEN AND WHERE?

Authorship

The writer of the Book of Ruth is anonymous. According to Jewish tradition,[1] Samuel wrote it as well as Judges. Modern Bible scholars are inclined to reject this idea, for Ruth 4:17–22 traces the descendants of Boaz and Ruth to David, and Samuel died before David ascended the throne (1 Sam. 25:1).

Before we dismiss Samuel's involvement too quickly, let us recall that the events of the Book of Ruth are set in the time of the judges (1:1), and that Samuel was both a prophet and a judge. The Book of Judges closes with an "appendix" (Judg. 17–21), in which we are given a glimpse of the spiritual and moral conditions of this era. Chapters 17 and 18 describe Israel's spiritual apostasy and show how rife was her infidelity. Chapters 19 through 21 describe the nadir of the people's moral degradation, recording their unbridled desire for revenge. Both stories concern the village of "Bethlehem in Judah" (Judg. 17:7–9; 19:2–18) and much of the contents of the Book of Ruth are enacted in this city. It should not surprise us, therefore, if the author of Judges also wrote the Book of Ruth.

Others object to Samuel's possible authorship on the grounds that the genealogy at the end of the book is "intended to show how the ancestors of the great king walked uprightly before God and man in piety of life."[2] They also find evidence, and rightfully so, of the composition of the book *after* the events it describes (cf. 1:1; 4:7, as well as 4:18–22). How much later still needs to be determined.

In the interest of an objective investigation and evaluation of the facts, let it be remembered that David is *not* spoken of as being king in 4:22. Samuel did anoint him to be king in the place of Saul even though it was more than ten years before he ascended the throne (1 Sam. 16:12–14).

Furthermore, the removal of the shoe in 4:7 is supposedly referring to a long unused custom. This custom is described in Deuteronomy 25:9–10, which Moses penned before the Israelites entered the Promised Land (1400 B.C.).[3] According to C. F. Keil, the first mention of the custom in Deuteronomy preceded its use in Ruth by 150 to 180 years.

Further evidence that must be weighed comes from the Books of Samuel. They contain no particulars respecting the ancestry of David, even though a genealogy was frequently given Hebrew kings. What could better explain the omission of David's genealogy in 1 Samuel than the fact that such data had already been given in the Book of Ruth?

In the final analysis, the internal evidence gives no indication of authorship,[4] but it does point to a date of composition much earlier than generally allowed by some Bible scholars.

Date

The Old Testament scholar C. F. Keil assigned the date to the period of the early monarchy, as did R. K. Harrison and E. J. Young.[5] Other writers prefer a date between David's reign and the Babylonian captivity (971–605 B.C.). Various possibilities are suggested: the "Solomonic enlightenment," the reign of Hezekiah, or a time immediately following the death of Athaliah.[6] A few writers believe the book was written during the exilic period (605–536 B.C.)[7]; the majority, however, favor a post-exilic date (538–400 B.C.).[8]

Cornill provides a succinct summary of the arguments in favor of a late date:

> Other grounds exist which favour a later time as the time of its composition. The time-indication in the days when the judges judged (i.1) presupposes the rigidly fixed chronological system of the Deuteronomic Exile History of Israel. The language of the book is strongly tinged with Aramaisms, and has many peculiarities which point with convincing and cogent force to the post-exilic period; while, on the other hand, the recital itself is mainly composed of reminiscences of older historical works, especially J [the "Yahwistic" or "Jehovistic" writer]. Quite a striking and convincing example is to be seen in Ruth iv. 7 compared with Deut. xxv. 9; here a custom which was current in the times of Deuteronomy is expressly explained as if it were an antiquarian curiosity. The conclusion (iv. 18–22), which displays the schematic arrangement of the genealogies of P [the "Priestly" writer], had better be left out of the account, because it may have been added later as the completion of vs. 12.[9]

J. Myers, on the other hand, lists a series of *archaic* Hebrew forms,[10] and these are difficult to reconcile with a late date of composition.

G. Gerleman likewise takes issue with those who wish to see several stages in the transmission of the book, or who for slender reasons persist in ignoring the historical evidence for an earlier date. He states:

> One could no longer talk about David and his lineage in the exilic period in such an unbiased fashion as it happens in the story of Ruth. . . . It must have been a very definite and compelling reason which caused the writer of Ruth to tell his story. . . . The notice, which connects David with Boaz and Ruth, is no secondary addition to an old story. On the contrary, this seemingly casual notice is to be viewed as an original kernel for which reason the Ruth story was written.[11]

Although I disagree with Gerleman as to his understanding of the purpose of the Book of Ruth, his argument from Israel's history and his defense of the unity of the original composition are helpful. If the Book of Ruth had *not* been based on a true and contemporary account of actual events, it would *never* have been invented in later days. The hatred of Moab, which was felt by the people of Israel and expressed by the prophets (Amos 2:8–9; Jer. 48; Ezek. 25:8–11), would *never* have allowed their greatest king to be thought of as descending from a Moabite woman.

The problem associated with the "antiquarian" interest (particularly as seen in 4:1–12) really surrounds the dating of the Book of Deuteronomy. If this work is assigned to Moses and written shortly before 1400 B.C., then sufficient time elapsed for the teachings of Moses to become obscured and for the Word of the Lord to be forgotten. It must be remembered that with a central sanctuary in which the Ark of the Covenant was kept, and with it the only extant copy of God's Word, the people were totally dependent on the ministry of the priests and Levites for instruction. As the religious leaders became apostate after the time of Joshua and the elders who outlived him, judges had to be raised up to bring the people back to the ways of the Lord. If the events of the Book of Ruth are assigned to the early period of Gideon's life (c. 1191–1151 B.C.),[12] then fully two centuries elapsed following the penning of Deuteronomy. This allows ample time for certain customs to fall into disuse.

Second, growing out of the assigning of documentary sources (J, E, D, and P) to many of the books of the Old Testament, it is not surprising that Bible critics see the Book of Ruth as supposedly containing evidence of Yahwistic (J) and Priestly (P) influence. Of this negative trend in biblical criticism, Samuel M. Zwemer had this to say:

> One reads with astonishment how the simple Scripture narrative was made both incredible and unintelligible in their [i.e., the redactor's, editor's, or reviser's] hands. Their method was by pedantic analysis, illogical presumptions, and anti-supernatural bias to refuse any quarter to the inspired writers.[13]

Even Winston Churchill, as learned a literary genius as ever lived, denounced this approach to the study of Scripture. He remarked:

> We reject with scorn all these learned and labored myths. . . . We believe that the most scientific view, the most up-to-date and rationalistic conception, will find its fullest satisfaction in taking the Bible literally. . . . We may be sure that all things happened just as they are set out according to Holy Writ. The impressions these people received were faithfully recorded and have been transmitted across the centuries with far more accuracy than many of the telegraphed accounts of goings-on today. In the words of a forgotten work of Mr. Gladstone, we rest with assurance on "the impregnable rock of Holy Scripture." Let the learned men of science and learning expand their knowledge . . . and prove with their research every detail of the records which have been preserved for us from those dim ages. All they will do is to fortify the grand simplicity and essential accuracy of the recorded truths which have lighted so far the pilgrimage of man.[14]

Other arguments in favor of a late date for the Book of Ruth are (1) its place in the third division of the Hebrew Bible (with the *Megilloth*), and (2) the claim that the book was written to combat the supposed "exclusivism" of Ezra and Nehemiah. These criticisms will be discussed below in the sections on the canonicity of Ruth and the intention of God behind the composition of the book.

For our purpose, after having duly consulted the writings of biblical scholars, there seems to be no reason for not assigning the writing of this pastoral idyll to the period following David's anointing by Samuel, or early in his reign in Hebron. We would date the events of chapter 1 as possibly transpiring between 1198 and 1185 B.C. (during the Midianite oppression that lasted from 1198–1191

B.C.). The written record could easily have been made between 1025 and 1005 B.C., if not by Samuel, then perhaps by Nathan or someone attached to David's court.

The place of writing is unknown and would obviously be associated with the author: Ramah, if Samuel wrote it; any one of David's residences if composed during his "outlaw" years; or Hebron if during his early reign.

Having considered the difficulties surrounding the authorship and date of the Book of Ruth—difficulties made even more perplexing by the many speculative views held by Bible scholars—we now need to consider the canonicity of Ruth and the place of the book in the Hebrew Bible. As we do so, we will find how important this subject is and why it has led certain writers to assign Ruth a late date of composition.

THE QUESTION OF QUALITY

The word *canon* (from the Greek *kanon,* meaning "rule"[15]) may possibly have been derived from the Semitic *qäneh,* "measuring rod." In the course of time, the term was used to designate the sum total of those books of the Old Testament that were qualitatively considered sacred by the Hebrews.

Shortly before the dawn of the Christian era, the Jews began referring to their sacred writings as those books that "defile the hands."[16] What this Semiticism originally signified, no one definitely knows.

It is possible that a passage of Scripture like Leviticus 16:24 contains a hint as to the meaning of this expression. According to this portion of the Law, the high priest on the Day of Atonement washed not only when he put on the garments of his office, *but also when he took them off.* Quite possibly, therefore, the expression "to defile the hands," when used in connection with God's holy Word, signified that the hands that had touched the sacred writings must first be washed before touching anything else. If this was not done, then the conditions surrounding the ceremonial purity of the Scriptures might not be maintained.

Dispute over Numbers

The number of books comprising the Hebrew canon are variously given as twenty-two and twenty-four. Josephus, a Jewish historian of the first century A.D., in handing down the tradition of his people, says:

> For we have not an innumerable multitude of books among us, dis-
> agreeing from and contradicting one another [as the Greeks have],
> but only twenty-two, which contain the records of all the past times;
> which are justly believed to be divine; and of them, five belong to
> Moses, which contain the laws, and the traditions of the origin of
> mankind till his death . . . but as to the time from the death of Moses
> till the reign of Artaxerxes, king of Persia, who reigned after Xerxes,
> the prophets, who were after Moses, wrote down what was done in
> their time in thirteen books. The remaining four books contain hymns
> to God, and precepts for the conduct of human life. It is true that our
> history has been written since Artaxerxes, very particularly, but has
> not been esteemed of the like authority with the former by our fore-
> fathers. . . .[17]

In Josephus's enumeration, Judges and Ruth were evidently counted as one book, and Jeremiah and Lamentations as one as well.[18] The Talmud and the Midrash list twenty-four books. In these lists, Ruth is separated from Judges, and Lamentations from Jeremiah.

The inclusion of the Book of Ruth in the canon has never been seriously questioned. Its *place* in the canon, however, has been the subject of endless debate.

Early Subdivisions

According to Josephus, the division of the Hebrew canon was threefold:[19]

As early as the translation of the Hebrew Scriptures into Greek (i.e., the Septuagint or LXX, c. 260 B.C.), the Book of Ruth occupied a place between Judges and 1 Samuel.[20] This was verified by Melito of Sardis (died c. A.D. 190).[21] Further evidence for including Ruth with the writings of the Former Prophets comes from a very old Hebrew-Aramaic enumeration of the books of the Old Testament. Listed as MS 54 of the library of the Greek patriarchate in Jerusalem, this old manuscript may be the oldest listing of the canonical books available.[22] The order, insofar as it concerns our present study, is: Genesis, Exodus, Leviticus, Joshua, Deuteronomy, Numbers, Ruth, Job, Judges. The important point to notice is that Ruth was included

The Books of the Hebrew Old Testament

LAW	PROPHETS		WRITINGS
	FORMER	LATTER	Poetical
Genesis—	Joshua—	Isaiah—	Five Rolls
Deuteronomy	II Kings	Malachi	Historical

with the historical books of the Old Testament and *not* with the "Writings."

The biblical scholar, Jerome (c. A.D. 340–420), who lived for many years in Antioch and spent the last thirty-five years of his life in Bethlehem, knew of the twenty-two book arrangement (referred to by Josephus). He is the first to refer to the *Kethûbim*, or "Writings,"[23] as a distinct part of the canon. The gathering together of these books of the Old Testament into a distinct group is, therefore, of late origin.

But what significance does all this have to the Book of Ruth?

Origin of our Mythconceptions

Because the Jews, in about the 4th century A.D., placed certain books together in a group so that they could be used at different festivals, modern scholars have assigned the writing of Ruth to a date much later than the biblical evidence warrants. Their reasoning runs something like this: "Ruth cannot have been written until *after* the 'canon of the prophets' had closed. Therefore an early date of composition is out of the question."[24] And with the assigning of a late date comes the distortion of the purpose or theme of the book.

In defense of the late date, and in an endeavor to preserve the authenticity of those books included in the Hebrew Bible, those who adhere to this view invariably claim that the issue of canonicity was not finally settled until the Council of Jamnia (A.D. 90).[25]

In response to this assertion, and in full realization that the position presented here is a minority one, an illustration of the early recognition that "God has spoken" comes from the Book of Habakuk (c. 615 B.C.). In chapter 1, the prophet is given a vision of

Judah's pending destruction at the hand of the Chaldeans (vv. 5–11).
In chapter 2, he is told to inscribe the message of the Lord on
tablets, that the one who reads it may take warning and flee the city
(v. 2).

If we are to apply artificial criteria of canonicity to this portion of
God's Word, then the word of the Lord through Habakkuk was not
received by the Jews as authoritative until formally designated as
"defiling the hands." This did not happen until much later when the
"canon of the prophets" was closed. By this time it would have been
too late for anyone to take warning (for Nebuchadnezzar took the
city in 605 B.C.).

It seems preferable, on biblical grounds, to conclude that the
pious in Israel recognized instinctively that God had spoken on
either hearing or reading his Word. Scripture, therefore, was immediately accepted as normative by those who were God-fearing. It
was not necessary for them to wait for some council to pass its
approval before the books of the Old Testament could be regarded
as authoritative.

What then may be said to have happened at Jamnia? Nothing is
known for certain. According to the Talmud and Mishnah, the canonicity of Ezekiel, Proverbs, Song of Solomon, and Esther was discussed by the scholars living in the city.[26] It seems preferable to
conclude with the late Merrill F. Unger that, whatever may have
transpired, "official sanction (i.e., canonization) did *not* create public opinion. It merely confirmed it."[27]

With these considerations in mind, we believe that the Book of
Ruth, as with any other portion of Scripture, would have been recognized as sacred as soon as it was written. This being the case, we
can approach the text and investigate the theme of the book un-
troubled by doubts raised by negative biblical criticism.

THE HEART OF THE MATTER

The confusion surrounding the date of the composition of Ruth
has carried over into, and obscured, its purpose. Those who hold to
a postexilic date see the book as a polemic against the supposedly
harsh, authoritarian practices of Ezra and Nehemiah. Others, who
pick up on the repeated emphasis of Ruth being a Moabitess, see in
the book a "tract for the times," rebuking Judah's exclusivism. A
large number of scholars believe that the whole book existed for the

sole purpose of supplying Israel with David's genealogy. A significant number, however, who espouse a negative approach to biblical criticism, deny the authenticity of the genealogy in 4:17–22.

A small number of writers hold to the theory that the Book of Ruth was written as a Midrash on a Bethlehem fertility-cult myth in which Elimelech represented the dying God, Naomi the mother-goddess, and Ruth her devotee.[28]

Still others believe the central theme of the story to be loyalty within the family, or the friendship of two women, or extolling the providence of God. These will all be dealt with as space permits. It is sufficient to say here that there seems to be confusion between the singular purpose of the book and its many subordinate themes. A work of literary merit can have only one central theme even though many important lessons may be gleaned from it. Oswald Loretz rightly observed:

> Exegesis has been thus far unable to supply a completely satisfactory answer to the most important question concerning the book of Ruth: what is its basic spirit or purpose? When one examines the literature that has appeared on Ruth, and takes special notice of the sections dealing with the book's author, he soon realizes how divided are the opinions of exegetes on this question. Thus, the opinion has been expressed that the book of Ruth is essentially a product of the story-teller's art.[29]

In Praise of Rhetoric

Richard Moulton was outspoken in his praise of the composition of Ruth. He wrote, "So delicate in its transparent simplicity, [is this book] that the worst service one can do the story is to comment on it."[30]

To adequately comment on so perfect a literary product is impossible, yet expounding its theme is a must for every Bible student. Its truth must be unraveled, understood, and shared, or else we will suffer the consequences of our neglect.

But how are we to understand this story? Is it a folktale, a pleasing pastoral idyll with little or no factual basis?

Jack Sasson has propounded a theory that deals with the literary genre of Ruth. He says:

> On the assumption that literature is never created in a vacuum, literary critics of the past century have begun to identify patterns in order

to isolate narrative elements common to a wide variety of literature. Such enterprises were essentially reductionistic even as they were integrative and holistic.[31]

Sasson then compares various schools of literary thought. He finally advocates a morphological approach based on the syntagmatic analysis of the structuralist school. His acceptance of the character and development of the plot necessitated by this viewpoint—one demanding a villain, a donor-helper, a sought-for person, the sought-for person's father, a dispatcher, a hero, and a false hero—imports to the narrative characters and elements from fiction that are totally foreign to the story. We may, therefore, dismiss his theory without further comment.

Among those scholars who appreciate the literary excellence of Ruth is S. R. Driver. He observed:

> The narrator manifestly takes delight in the graceful and attractive details of his picture. His principal characters are amiable, God-fearing, courteous, unassuming; and all in different ways show how a religious spirit may be carried unostentatiously into the conduct of daily life.[32]

Although we may praise the literary excellence of the writer of this book, plainly the story involves more than perfection of form.

A Way of Life

Driver's observation has led several writers to believe that the central theme or purpose of the Book of Ruth is the exemplary conduct of the leading characters: Naomi, Ruth, Boaz.

Some students of the Scriptures point out that the story begins and ends with Naomi (1:6ff.; 4:14–17) and believe that she is the central figure.[33] Others regard the theme as being a story of two women.[34] Still others view the contents as descriptive of ideal widowhood.[35]

I. Bettan sees the all-embracing theme of the book as the law of humankindness that transcends national boundaries.[36] L. Ryken takes this theme even further and shows how Ruth's love for Naomi led to her marriage to Boaz so that she could fulfill her duty to her mother-in-law.[37]

Keil and Delitzsch link the theme of exemplary conduct with the genealogy that concludes the book and, by partly quoting K. A. Auberlen and by blending their thoughts with his, affirm:

"The book of Ruth contains, as it were, the inner side, the spiritually moral background of the genealogies which play so significant a part even in the Israelitish antiquity"; so much is unquestionably true, that the book contains a historical picture from the family life of the ancestors of David, intended to show how the ancestors of this great king walked uprightly before God and man in piety and singleness of heart, and in modesty and purity of life. "Ruth, the Moabitish great-great-grandmother of David, longed for the God and people of Israel with all the deepest earnestness of her nature, and joined herself to them with all the power of love; and Boaz was an upright Israelite, without guile, full of holy reverence for every ordinance of God and man, and full of benevolent love and friendliness towards the poor heathen woman. From such ancestors was the man descended in whom all the nature of Israel was to find its royal concentration and fullest expression."[38]

G. Campbell Morgan enlarges on this theme by claiming that two permanent values can be found in this short story: (1) the secrets of saintship, for God is the sufficiency of trusting souls; and (2) the values of saintship, in that trusting souls are the instruments of God. He continues:

A saint is a person separated to the will of God. Ruth and Boaz lived the life of saintship in circumstances of the utmost difficulty, finding their sufficiency for such a life in God.

Ruth was a Moabitess, of an accursed race . . . [who] came back with Naomi into poverty, and to a people who in all probability were hostile to them both. Thus the saintship of Ruth was in spite of difficulties, and flourished amid circumstances calculated to discourage her.

Boaz lived amid people of privilege in times of degeneracy . . . he was a mighty man of wealth, and consequently able to procure whatever would contribute to the case of his material existence. That condition is always perilous to a life of faith. . . .[39]

Morgan summarizes the character of Ruth and Boaz in the following way:

Ruth was a woman capable of love, characterized by modesty, of fine gentleness, of splendid courage; a woman in all the grace and beauty of womanhood. Boaz was a man of integrity, of courtesy, of tender passion, of courage; a man in all the strength and glory of manhood.[40]

These viewpoints have much to commend them, but we must ask, is this what God intended to reveal in and through this brief story? Is this the central theme of the book, or merely one of its lessons?

Keil and Delitzsch believe that the central theme is the link between the past and the future. They state with confidence, "the meaning and tendency of the whole narrative is brought clearly to light. The genealogical proof of the descent of David from Perez through Boaz and the Moabitess, Ruth (chap. iv. 18–22), forms not only the end, but the starting point, of the history contained in the book."[41]

Unresolved Tension

I believe that the concluding section to this short story is authentic, although many reputable scholars believe it is a later addition.[42] It is somewhat ironic to find some "liberal" critics, defendants of the late date, affirming the genuineness of the last paragraph while many of their colleagues deny its authenticity, claiming that the genealogy was copied from 1 Chronicles 2:12–15 by an editor.

A. Jepsen stresses the comfort the genealogy brings and shows how hopelessness was turned to hope and then to triumphant assurance as Ruth gave birth to Obed.[43] R. Hals states that "the story has a theological purpose which pervaded the entire book, namely, to bear witness to God's hidden control of history by tracing his hand in the ancestry of David."[44]

But is this *all* we are intended to understand from our study of this exquisite piece of literature? Would anyone have taken the trouble to write an account of obscure people if all he intended to do was record for posterity a genealogy? Leon Morris rightly observes, "The genealogy appears rather as an appendix than as a climax."[45]

How then are we to understand this pastoral story? Some have suggested its purpose is polemical. Others believe it was written to promote religious zeal. Still others look on it as advocating a return to familial responsibilities. A more recent view builds its theme on certain literary and psychological elements inherent in the text. And then there are those who see in the book a theological principle. We will summarize each of these viewpoints.

Seeds of Corruption

Those who see in the Book of Ruth a protest against the supposedly rigid conditions enforced by Ezra and Nehemiah,[46] or the
evils of Athaliah's reign, build their case largely on the fact that Ruth
is frequently referred to as "the Moabitess" (1:4, 22; 2:2, 6, 11–13, 21;
4:5, 10). Their theories are also conditioned by their dating of this
book (i.e., after the exile if written against Ezra and Nehemiah[47]; or
during the latter part of the divided monarchy if directed against the
practices of Athaliah[48]).

B. Vellas succinctly rebuts the case for the former view:

> A book which was written in those troubled times of Ezra and Nehe-
> miah, as a protest against those men, could not possess that beautiful
> atmosphere and those idyllic surroundings which, so skillfully, the
> author of Ruth creates, nor could it be possible to possess an un-
> forced, serene and calm tone of style.[49]

Likewise, belief that the book was written as a polemic against the
evils of Athaliah's reign has to create from the history of the times a
context in which to fit the story. Then, when this has been done, the
tenor of the book refuses to accommodate itself to that era.

Unassigned Frequency

Some Jewish interpreters see in the Book of Ruth a tract written
to promote religious zeal. Ruth the Moabitess is held up as an example of the perfect proselyte.[50] D. Harvey writes, "The emphasis of
the book is not so much on Ruth's devotion to her mother-in-law,
as on the fact that Ruth was accepted in Israel in spite of her for-
eignness."[51]

The emphasis of the book, however, does appear to be placed on
Ruth's avowal of loyalty to her mother-in-law (1:16–17); willingness
to support her (chap. 2); and devotion, even to the extent of marrying a kinsman and bearing a child for Naomi when, it was freely
acknowledged, she could have had any man of her choosing in
Bethlehem (3:10–13).

If we are to see anything striking in Ruth's conduct, it would be
her love for and kindness to Naomi—kindness above and beyond
conventional duty. This led one rabbinic commentator to believe
that the theme of the book is to teach "how great is the reward that

accrues to those who perform kindly deeds" (*Midrash Rabbah,* Ruth 2:14).

The theme of familial responsibility, therefore, would seem to warrant further consideration.

The Cost Factor

Those who believe that the Book of Ruth was designed to promote a resurgence of interest in levirate marriages stress the conduct of Boaz, who performed this rite even though he was not under legal obligation to do so. They emphasize his magnanimity, whereas his unnamed kinsman probably refused to marry Ruth because of the financial cost involved in supporting both her and Naomi.

Vellas, who dates the book in the postexilic period, sees the purpose of the writer as stressing the sacredness of family bonds in an age when, as he believes Malachi 3:24 shows, these bonds were being relaxed.[52] J. P. Hyatt accepts this thesis and argues for a wider interpretation and application of levirate marriages.[53] H. H. Rowley is a little more cautious. He agrees that the story of Ruth's marriage is generally linked with the issue of levirate marriage, but admits that "this is not strictly a case of levirate marriage, since Boaz is not a brother-in-law."[54]

Although levirate marriage is illustrated in Genesis 38 (which antedates the time of Moses), the custom receives specific legislative significance in Deuteronomy 25:5–10. S. R. Driver, however, rejects all thought of levirate marriage and states that Boaz "purchased" Ruth.[55]

In light of the differences about the purpose of Ruth, a commentator must be careful not to build too much on one viewpoint of the book.

The Reward of the Righteous

Closely associated with the relationship of the historical and cultural approach of this interesting story and the perplexing problems surrounding the purpose of Ruth is a view that develops the writer's thought around the ideas of emptiness and fullness. This approach to the theme of Ruth is both literary and psychological in its scope.

In chapter 1, for example, we are introduced to a family enduring the hardship created by continuous famine. They migrate to Moab and there Naomi's husband dies. As the writer reminds his readers, she is bereft. Later on, her sons die, and we are told that now she is bereft of her husband and her two sons. Naomi hears that the Lord has visited his people in giving them bread. Here, it is believed by advocates of this approach, the author introduces the theme of fullness. "And they came to Bethlehem at the beginning of the barley harvest" rounds out the cycle.

The succeeding sections of the Book of Ruth do not lend themselves as clearly or as readily to the idea of emptiness and fullness, even though hunger is present and Ruth (with help from Boaz) fends for herself and returns heavy-laden to her mother-in-law (chap. 2).

Chapter 3 has even less of the emptiness and fullness motif, although it does end with Boaz's words to Ruth, "Do not go empty to your mother-in-law" (3:17).

Chapter 4 takes on the note of triumph and celebration. It also turns the spotlight back on Naomi, for she takes Obed and becomes his nurse.[56]

We are left with the impression in this view that western patterns of plot development (emptiness-fullness) are being imposed on an eastern story. The result is rather like trying to force one's foot into a shoe that, for all its good appearance, is of the wrong size.

Of a similar nature is the theory that the theme surrounds the continuance of a family and the perpetuation of its name. In this view, Elimelech's line was threatened with extinction. Naomi was past childbearing years. The outlook was hopeless. Through the wife of one of Elimelech's deceased sons, a child is born into the home, and this child is reckoned to Naomi. In time he becomes the grandfather of David—an event so momentous as to ensure the family an endless succession and a never-ending renown.[57]

Those who adhere to this view of the purpose of Ruth place emphasis on the repeated references to Elimelech (e.g., 2:3; 4:9–10) and the fact that God, in his mercy, has not withdrawn his loving-kindness from the living and the dead (cf. 2:20).

There is much historical validity to this approach, but the question remains: Is the importance of the perpetuation of the family the key theme of the book? If so, then what long-lasting lesson are we to learn from it?

Perhaps W. Rudolph best stated the book's purpose, "Ruth, like the major part of the Old Testament literature, does not speak of men but of God; its purpose is not that we should admire a gallery of noble people, but that we should learn how God acts."[58] Leon Morris confirms this approach. He says, "This book is a book about God. He rules over all and brings blessings to those who trust Him."[59]

The Glory of Grace

In reviewing the teaching of this book on the person of God, Rudolph believes that the central theme is one of extolling God's providence and loving-kindness.[60] Jepsen sees it as implying hope.[61] Josephus, the Jewish historian, in giving his reason for including the Book of Ruth in his *Antiquities of the Jews*, says:

> I was therefore obliged to relate this history of Ruth, because I had a mind to demonstrate the power of God, who, without difficulty, can raise those that are of ordinary parentage to dignity and splendor, to which he advanced David, though he were born of mean parents (V.ix.4).

Morris responds:

> It is better to see [the book] as a tale told because it is true and because it shows something of the relationship between God and man. There is a good deal to be said for the view that the key verse is 2:12, "The Lord recompense thy work, and a full reward be given thee of the Lord God of Israel, under whose wings thou art come to trust" (AV). That is what the book is about. Ruth takes the initiative in chapter 2, Naomi in chapter 3, and Boaz in chapter 4, but the book is not really about any of them. The implication throughout is that God is watching over His people, and that He brings to pass what is good.[62]

Although I do not wish to disagree with many competent expositors who take other viewpoints, it seems that the Book of Ruth emphasizes the *grace of God.*

God *in his grace* allows Elimelech to go to Moab in order to escape the famine. The temporary stay becomes a permanent residency there, and in the course of time both of Elimelech's sons marry Moabite women (1:1–5). Following the death, first of her husband and then of her sons, Naomi decides to return to Bethlehem. The reason given in the text is that she has heard, even in Moab, that God in his grace has visited his people in giving them food (1:6).

Naomi returns to her native village. When the people of the town come out to see her, she laments God's treatment of her. Her thoughts are all of herself and her plight (1:19–21). No mention is made of Ruth who, as a recent convert of the grace of God, will prove to be to Naomi better than seven sons (4:15). Furthermore, God has graciously brought Naomi and Ruth back to Judah at the beginning of the barley harvest (1:22). They will not starve.

In chapter 2, Ruth goes to glean in the field and happens "by chance" to ask for permission to work in a section of the field belonging to Boaz. Many expositors see this incident as a further evidence of God's gracious care of her and provision for her need. Boaz pronounces a benediction on her (2:12), and this blessing comes true sooner than either of them expect.

At the end of the harvest season, Naomi suggests to Ruth that she lay claim to an old Hebrew custom and request Boaz to provide "rest" for her (chap. 3). This "rest" is with a husband and in the home he will provide. Here again we see something of the gracious provision of God for his people (Deut. 25:5–10).

Finally, in chapter 4, we see someone who, as a stranger, was excluded from the commonwealth of Israel. As an alien to the covenants of promise, she was formerly without hope and without God, yet now through grace is redeemed and accepted by the people of Bethlehem. She finds hope and security in their city, marries, bears a son, and becomes not only the great-grandmother of David but also a direct ancestor of the Lord Jesus Christ himself.

Keil and Delitzsch unwittingly reinforce this idea of the grace of God by emphasizing the "messianic trait" in the genealogy of 4:18–22. Ruth is the "tribe-mother of the great and pious David, on account of her faithful love to the people of Israel, and her entire confidence in Jehovah, the God of Israel."[63]

Many lessons can be gleaned from the story of Ruth, but the central theme of the book is the grace of God and the blessings of obedience. Such a literary purpose best fits the content of the book.

NOTES

Introduction

1. Cf. J. Lilley, "Ruth," *ZPEB*, 5:176.
2. Cf. Harrison, p. 1059.
3. Hermann Gunkel, *Die Religion in Geschichte und Gegenwart* (Göttingen: Vandenhoeck and Ruprecht, 1916), 4, col. 2181, and Robert H. Pfeiffer, *Introduction to the Old Testament* (New York: Harper and Brothers, 1941), p. 718; both denied that the events of the Book of Ruth were historical. H. H. Rowley, however, in *Growth of the Old Testament* (London: Hutchinson's U. Library, 1950), p. 150, accepts the historicity of the events even though he does not believe that the book was written until the postexilic period.
4. James Morison, *Ruth*, The Pulpit Commentary (New York: Funk and Wagnalls, n.d.), p. ii.

Chapter 1

1. *The Thurber Carnival* (New York: Modern Library, 1957), pp. 47–51.
2. This *waw* consecutive is frequently translated "now." Because here it is connected to the imperfect, some Bible scholars have assumed that the Book of Ruth was originally part of another work. This common construction is also found at the beginning of Leviticus, Numbers, Joshua, Judges, 1 Samuel, 2 Kings, 2 Chronicles, Nehemiah, Esther, and the prophecy of Ezekiel.
3. "Bethlehem-judah" is a specific term used by the historian to distinguish this small Judean town from the larger and better known (at that time) city in Zebulun (Josh. 19:15; see also Mic. 5:2).
4. A large number of expositors believed that the famine of Ruth 1 is to be dated at the time of the Midianite and Amalekite invasion when these peoples came up "as grasshoppers for multitude, to destroy the land" (see Judg. 6).
5. The scene was described eloquently by Cox, pp. 44–48.
6. The writer specifically used the term "the fields of Moab" (1:1–2, 6). Had he so desired, he could have employed the word *'ereṣ*, "land" (cf. 1:7 where *'ereṣ* was used to describe "the land of Judah"). His emphasis of the "fields," therefore, was deemed to be intentional.
7. See Morris, pp. 249f.; Cox, p. 45.
8. Hebrew names in antiquity often reflected the religious connections of one's parents or were given to a child because the parents discerned a

characteristic in their son or daughter which brought some name to mind. Recent studies have shown that names ending in *melek* were invariably held by people of noble descent. The names given Mahlon and Chilion occur in literature outside the Bible. The reason these names were given, and their significance, is still a matter of conjecture. See Sasson, pp. 18f. The explanation of W. E. Staples, "The Book of Ruth," *AJSL* 53 (1937), pp. 145–57, that the names of all the members indicated a connection with the fertility cult, lacks credibility.

9. The change in the verb from *gûr*, "to sojourn (as an alien)," to *way-yihyû*, "to remain there" was most significant and indicated a change in the original plan. (In v. 4 further regression is evident. Following the death of Elimelech, the sons settled [*wayyēšebû*, "to dwell"] in Moab. The ten years they spent in Moab gave proof of the fact that they had no real thought of returning to Judah. Then they too died.)

10. Psychologists have discerned that for a person to feel secure enough to settle in a given place he or she needs to experience a sense of belonging, worth, and competence. See the excellent articles by Gary H. Strauss, "What Really Happened in Eden?" *Psychology for Living* (Dec. 1976), pp. 18–19; (Jan. 1977), pp. 16–17; and (Feb. 1977), pp. 16–17. Both Elimelech and Naomi must have experienced this, for he decided "to remain" in Moab (changing his earlier plan), and she decided to remain in this foreign land even after her husband died.

11. Cox, p. 53.

12. Fuller, p. 23.

13. The Hebrew construction of 1:3 is unusual. See Morris, p. 250.

14. The Midrash made Ruth the daughter of Eglon, king of Moab. This claim was without substance. It has been accepted, however, by Geoffrey T. Bull, *Love Song in Harvest* (London: Pickering & Inglis, 1972), pp. 18ff.

15. Morris (pp. 250–51) had some sage comments on the meanings of these names.

16. *Talmud*, Baba Bathra, 91*a*.

17. Cf. God's dealings with Jonah in C. J. Barber and G. H. Strauss, *The Effective Parent* (San Bernardino, Calif.: Here's Life, 1980), pp. 3–81.

18. Cf. Deuteronomy 1:8; 3:20; 4:5, 14; 5:31; 6:1, 10, 18, 23; 7:13; 8:1; 9:5; 10:11; 11:9–12, 21; 12:1; 15:4; 19:2, 8, 14; 25:19; 26:3. See P. D. Miller, Jr., "The Gift of God," *Interpretation* 28 (1969), pp. 451–65.

19. See R. Morosco, "Theological Implications of Fear," *Journal of Psychology and Theology* 1, 2 (1973), pp. 43–50.

20. These criteria were based on Paul's distinctions in 1 Corinthians 8:1–11:1. They may be studied in Charles R. Erdman's delightful little commentary *The First Epistle to the Corinthians* (Philadelphia: Westminster, 1927), pp. 75–96.

Chapter 2

1. C. J. Barber, *Vital Encounter* (San Bernardino, Calif.: Here's Life, 1979), pp. 123–32.
2. This definition has been adapted from John R. W. Stott's handling of *agapē* love in *The Epistles of John* (Grand Rapids: Eerdmans, 1964).
3. Cf. Deuteronomy 14:29; 16:11; 24:19; 26:12; Psalm 94:6 for special legislation designed to alleviate some of their distress. God made himself the protector of widows (Ps. 68:5) and executed justice on their behalf (Deut. 10:18; 27:19). His beneficent laws, however, were flouted (Ps. 94:6; Isa. 1:23; Mal. 3:5).
4. Morris has observed, "When God visits, everything depends on the state of affairs He finds. The verb is a warning against presuming on the holiness of God and a reminder that God delights to bless. On this occasion His visit means the end of famine. The bread now available is regarded as God's gift" (p. 252).
5. The question is naturally raised, Why should each return to the house of her *mother*? Were their fathers dead? Ruth 2:11 seems to imply that Ruth's father still is alive. Keil and Delitzsch conjectured that their mothers would know how to comfort them. Others believed that inherent in this verse we have evidence of a matriarchal system (see D. R. Mace, *Hebrew Marriage* [London: Hutchinson's U. Library, 1953], pp. 18ff.). Campbell listed reasons given by others as to why the young widows should return to their mothers' houses and concluded, based on evidence gleaned from Genesis 24 and the Song of Solomon (3:4 and 8:2), that "the 'mother's house' was the focus for matters pertinent to marriage, especially for discussion and planning for marriage" (p. 64). To this discussion should be added the weight of Morris's research and reflection: "In a polygamous society the place for such as Ruth and Orpah would be the women's quarters presided over by the mother" (p. 253).
6. For a discussion of *hesed* see *TWOT*, 1: 698–700; N. Glueck, *Hesed in the Bible* (Leiden: E. J. Brill, 1967); K. Sakenfeld, *The Meaning of Hesed in the Bible* (Missoula, Mont.: Scholars Press, 1978).
7. "With you," *'immākem*, is masculine, whereas we would have expected a feminine form. It is the first of seven instances where a masculine plural occurs with a feminine antecedent. (The second is "you have done" in this verse; then "to you," 1:9, 11; "than for you," 1:13; and "the two of them" 1:19b; 4:11). Joüon, *Grammaire* (#149b [pp.457–58]) believed that these masculine forms were evidence of the late date of composition of the Book of Ruth. Myers (p. 20) refuted this theory. Campbell (p. 65) concluded his review of the discussion by offering his own theory that this is an *early* Hebrew feminine dual suffix that ends

in -*m*, just as the masculine plural ending does, but contrasted with the feminine plural -*n*. One exception to this theory occurs in verse 19. A possible explanation is that this masculine usage may be a way of referring to corporate personality and be an evidence of *early* Hebrew philological history. See also Morris, p. 255f.

8. For a discussion of *menûḥâ*, "rest," see *TWOT*, 2:1323f.

9. Cox, pp. 65–67.

10. See Joüon, *Ruth*, p. 36; Morris, p. 254.

11. The usage of *kî*, here translated "no," has been challenged by some lexicographers and grammarians (see Koehler and Baumgartner's *Lexicon in Veteris Testamentum libros* [Leiden: E. J. Brill, 1951–1953], pp. 431–33; Joüon, *Ruth*, pp. 40–41). However, C. Brockelmann, *Hebräische Syntax* (Neukirchen, Kreis Moers: Verlag der Buchhandlung des Erzeinhungsvereins, 1956), #134*a*, and Kennedy, p. 16, were quite prepared to accept its adversative usage.

12. Naomi could obviously marry again. What she was alluding to here is her inability to bear children. See Morris, p. 257.

13. Campbell (p. 67) neatly identified the three parts to the protasis of Naomi's statement and then explained the apodosis.

14. The *halāhēn* of verse 13, "for them," has been widely regarded as an Aramaism and *ipso facto* evidence of the late date for the writing of Ruth. The pendulum of modern scholarly opinion is now swinging in the opposite direction and many are seeing the usage of this word as further evidence for the early composition of this book. Cf. Campbell, p. 68; Morris, p. 257. However, amending the text to *lāhēn* as some textual critics do is to resort to a highly questionable expedient.

15. Reference here was obviously to the practice of levirate marriage (Deut. 25:5–10). Cf. Leggett; H. H. Rowley, "The Marriage of Ruth," *HTR* 46 (1947), pp. 77–99; M. Burrows, "The Ancient Oriental Background of Levirate Marriage," *BASOR* 70 (1940), pp. 2–15; Mace, pp. 95–118; Neufeld, *Ancient Hebrew Marriage Laws* (1944), pp. 23–55; T. and D. Thompson, "Some Legal Problems in the Book of Ruth," *VT* 28 (1968), pp. 79–99; deVaux, *Ancient Israel* (1965) pp. 24–38, 521f.

16. See Gray, p. 410; *TWOT*, 1:132; J. J. M. Roberts, "The Hand of Yahweh," *VT* 21 (1971), pp. 244–51.

17. Watson, p. 376; see also George Lawson, *Exposition of the Book of Ruth* (Edinburgh: J. Ritchie, 1805), pp. 35ff.

18. Cox, pp. 68–70.

19. Campbell, p. 72. A "one-way" kiss of farewell was usual in stories of the conclusion of a relationship.

20. Watson, p. 376.

21. It has been conjectured that this oath was probably accompanied by some expressive gesture such as simulating one's throat being cut by

passing a finger across it. The formula for the oath Ruth used is found only here and in 1 Samuel 3:17; 14:44; 20:13; 25:22; 1 Kings 2:23; 20:10; 2 Kings 6:31.

22. Morris said: "As Ruth was much younger than Naomi and would probably live longer this implies that she will so identify herself with Naomi's community that she will stay on there after Naomi's death. The reference to burial seems scarcely to be needed, but we must bear in mind that for the ancient world proper burial was of great importance. . . . We should not overlook [Ruth's] use of the divine name 'Yahweh.' She does not invoke Chemosh or the gods generally. She has taken Yahweh to be her God and it is upon Him accordingly that she calls" (p. 261). See also Wright, p. 17.

23. Taylor (p. 23) has reminded us of Thomas Arnold, the great British educator, who first won the hearts of the young boys of Rugley College to himself, and then, when they had learned that they could trust him, he pointed them to the Savior (see A. P. Stanley's *Life and Correspondence of Thomas Arnold* [Boston: Fields, Osgood, n.d.]).

24. Watson, p. 379.

25. See Morris, "Additional Note," pp. 264–68.

26. The word order in the original shows the emphasis of Naomi's words. It may be rendered, "Full I went out, and empty [Yahweh] has brought me back." Naomi's *I* stands first in the sentence and *Yahweh* last, showing the polarization Naomi felt.

27. The feminine form of "and *they* said" shows that it was the women who were in the city and came out to greet Naomi. See KD, 4:476.

28. The Niphal of the root *hwm* gives evidence of the excitement of those in Bethlehem on recognizing Naomi (cf. 1 Sam. 4:5 and 1 Kings 1:45, where the same word is used). The delight of the women found no response in Naomi's heart. She was still mourning the loss of her loved ones.

29. Morris (pp. 264–68) has a good discussion of the meaning of *Shaddai*.

30. Taylor, pp. 25–26.

Chapter 3

1. Howard J. Ruff, *How to Prosper in the Coming Bad Years* (San Ramon, Calif.: Target, 1979), pp. 3–5.

2. Naomi alluded to this in verse 20, "Call me not Naomi . . . for the Almighty has dealt very bitterly with me. . . . the LORD has testified against me and the Almighty has afflicted me." Later, the rabbis coined a saying, "Whom the Lord loveth he maketh rich."

3. *Meyuddā'*, the Pual participle of *yd'*, "to know," referred in this context to a blood relative, acquaintance, or kinsman, someone from the same

tribe, but *not* a brother. Campbell (pp. 88–90) proposed changing the root *myd* to *mwd*, "covenant-brother," but he has been answered by Sasson (p. 39). Morris (p. 268) preferred the term "kinsman."

Those who see in the use of this word a "deliberate archaism" on the part of the biblical writer should reconsider the case for the true antiquity of the Book of Ruth. Driver pointed out that "the general Hebrew style (the idioms and syntax) shows no marks of deterioration . . . and stands on a level with the best parts of Samuel" (p. 454).

4. *Mimmišpat*, "of the family of," has posed problems for translators. Joüon, *Ruth* (p. 46), was of the opinion that the preposition should be translated "by," and that *mišpāḥāh* be given the force of "by the husband." But *mišpāḥāh* was regularly and consistently used of a subdivision of a tribe (e.g., "clan" or part of an extended family). See F. I. Andersen, "Israelite Kinship Terminology and Social Structure," *BT* 20 (1969), pp. 29–39; and deVaux, pp. 4–13.

5. See KD, "according to rabbinic tradition, which, however, is not well established, Boaz was the nephew of Elimelech" (4:477).

6. The term *'îš gibbôr ḥayil*, "a mighty man of valor," may best be likened to a medieval knight. He was a man who had proved his worth on the field of battle and, in the course of time, had accumulated a measure of wealth. Morris only partly agreed with this conclusion. He wrote, "[The term] applied originally to a man distinguished for military prowess, but it is now used widely of those whose excellence lies in other fields. In the Old Testament it most often has to do with fighting capacity. Boaz may have been a warrior, for these were troubled times and any man might have to fight. But in this book he appears rather as a solid citizen" (p. 269). See *TDOT*, 2:373–77.

7. See Judges 6:12; 11:1; 1 Samuel 9:1; 1 Kings 11:28; and 2 Kings 15:20, where *gibbôr ḥayil* is used.

8. Ruth's ethnic origin is kept constantly before the reader. This is not without significance, and the word "Moabitess" is accompanied by the article in five specific instances (1:22; 2:2, 21; 4:5, 10). The vulnerability of Ruth's situation is stressed in this chapter.

9. This word is in the singular. Taylor wrote, "The field to which Ruth went, though apparently one large and undivided area, was really made up of the aggregate portions of land possessed by those who dwelt in Bethlehem. Just as, even at the present day, in some parts of Switzerland the agricultural population live in villages round which their several patches of land lie—not cut up by hedges or fenced off by stone walls—but forming what appears to be one immense field, though it is actually very carefully mapped out and divided by landmarks which are perfectly recognizable by the inhabitants themselves; so it was, long ago, in Bethlehem. To a casual visitor there would seem to be but

one field, but yet the portion of each proprietor was marked sometimes by heaps of small stones, and sometimes by single upright stones placed at short but regular intervals from each other. This enables us to understand the precept against the removal of a neighbor's landmark, and explains why in the narrative before us the word 'field' is in the singular, and why it is said that Ruth found her place of privilege in the 'part of the field which belonged to Boaz'" (pp. 38–39).

10. *'Aḥar 'ašer 'emṣā'-ḥēn be'ênāyw*, "after him in whose eyes I shall find favor," has been variously interpreted. Campbell reminded us this was a frequently used idiom that "seems always to be used by a person of inferior status to a superior" (p. 92). The law, however, specifically stated that widows and foreigners were to be allowed to glean (Lev. 19:9ff.; 23:22; Deut. 24:19) for, as Morris observed, "Gleaning was not dependent on the whim of landowners" (p. 270). Ruth's discretion was seen in her willingness to persevere until she found a friendly landowner, someone who would look on her with favor.

11. This is a unique expression found only here and in Ecclesiastes 2:14–15.

12. See also C. Ellison, *Loneliness* (Chappaqua, N.Y.: Christian Herald, 1980); and H. C. Warlick's *Conquering Loneliness* (Waco, Tex.: Word, 1979).

13. See B. M. Newman and P. R. Newman, *Development Through Life* (Homewood, Ill.: Dorsey Press, 1975). I have added the element of *hope* for biblical reasons. Some psychologists may choose to look on this as actualization or assign it a term involving the concept of a future-orientation. It seems to me, however, that *hope* expresses the idea better, involving breadth (i.e., various areas of fulfillment) as well as depth (of experience), and all with a view to the appropriation of the truth.

14. Sasson offered the following interpretation of the events: "In 2:3b the narrator observes that Ruth 'happened to come to the part of the field belonging to Boaz.' In view of the story's stress on God's providential guiding of the lives of this family, it is surprising to find such a crucial item in the pattern of events that brought Ruth and Boaz together attributed to chance. Such a secular point of view is startling, to say the least. How can the same writer trace a chain of events whose beginning (1:6) and ending (4:13) are found in God's all-causality, and then describe one of the links in the middle of that chain as accidental? The answer, of course, lies in the subtlety of the writer's style. Surprising as it may seem at first glance, the author's real meaning in 2:3b is actually the opposite of what he says. The labeling of Ruth's meeting with Boaz as 'chance' is nothing more than the author's way of saying that no human intent was involved. For Ruth and Boaz it was an accident, but not for God. The tenor of the whole story makes it clear that the

narrator sees God's hand throughout. In fact, the very secularism of his expression here is his way of stressing that conviction. It is a kind of underplaying for effect. By calling this meeting an accident, the writer enables himself subtly to point out that even the 'accidental' is directed by God.

"Ruth had come with a request that could not be fulfilled by a mere overseer. All that he could do is ask her to step aside and wait until the 'boss' arrived. In this way Ruth was assured of meeting Boaz, since the latter could hardly fail to notice her as she stood by."

15. Cox, p. 88; Taylor, p. 46.
16. R. deVaux, *Early History of Israel*, pp. 717–27.
17. L. Kohlberg, *Collected Papers on Moral Development and Moral Education* (San Francisco: Harper & Row, 1973–), in process.
18. deVaux, pp. 30–35.
19. Taylor, pp. 37–38.
20. *Wehinnēh-bō'az bā'*, "And look, Boaz came," draws attention to the fact that the string of imperfects with the *waw*-consecutive (v. 3) is interrupted by the word *look*. It is a graphic and vivid way of focusing the reader's attention on something new that is taking place.
21. While some commentators have stated that there is no reason to see in these greetings an expression of a pious attitude (cf. H. Gunkel, *Ruth, Reden und Aufsätze* [1913], pp. 65–92), and have advanced as their reason the Arabic *Allah ma'akum* ("Allah be with you") and the answer *Allah yaḥphaḍak* ("may Allah protect you"), such reasoning fails to account for Boaz's use of the most revered name for God among the Hebrews: *Yahweh*. If *Elohim* had been used, we would concur with the weight of scholarly opinion.

But what are we to make of the response of the reapers (who also used the name *Yahweh*) and Boaz's subsequent statement to them to have a "hands off" policy where Ruth is concerned? Surely their standard of morality should be in keeping with their religious profession. A possible answer to this dilemma may be found in their evident courtesy. Boaz, their employer, uses a term implying great respect for God, and they may be using the same term out of respect for him.
22. See Morris, p. 271.
23. Sasson, p. 46.
24. There is no article with "Moabitess," and the overseer gave no name to the woman he was describing. By these gestures he implied, in his communication of the facts to Boaz, that she was insignificant and of no social account.
25. *Wattō'mer 'alaqoṭāh-nnā' we'āsaptî bā'omārîm 'aḥarēy haqqôṣerîm*, "And she asked, 'Please let me glean, and I will gather among the sheaves, after the reapers.'" Commentators have puzzled over Ruth's

request. To glean among the sheaves was not permitted, or was viewed as a special favor (see 2:15). Was this a problem of Ruth's dialect or did the overseer improperly understand Ruth's request? Was it possible that Ruth had a deficient understanding of what the Law permitted? Or was it that Ruth asked to be allowed to gather up what had been left behind by the reapers, working between the bound sheaves? Joüon, *Ruth* (p. 49), preferred to amend the text so that *'omārîm*, "sheaves," is changed to *'amîrîm*, "swath, row of fallen grain." Such attempts to explain interpretive problems inherent in the text are at best doubtful expedients.

26. *Mē'āz habbōqer we'ad-'attāh zeh*, "since the morning even until now" or "from early morning until now," is a temporal phrase. The question posed by grammarians is whether or not this phrase goes with the second part of the sentence. If so (and the pointing of the MT indicates that it should), then the emphasis is to be placed on the diligence with which Ruth stuck to her task.

27. See Cox, pp. 88–89.

28. What was the nature of this *habbayit*, "and she sat"? W. Reed, *College of the Bible Quarterly* 41 (1964), p. 8, believed it was a latrine. R. A. Knox, *The Old Testament, Newly Translated from the Vulgate* (New York: Sheed and Ward, 1948–50), 1:378, translated this as if Ruth had not returned to her home. It seems preferable to see this "shelter" as a temporary structure made of upright poles and roofed with branches or straw. Those in need of rest could sit in its shade.

29. See Gary H. Strauss, "What Ever Happened in Eden?" *Psychology for Living* 17 (December, 1976), pp. 18–19, for a discussion of the elements of our security, how these were lost at the time of the Fall, and the manner in which they are restored to us when we believe in Christ.

Chapter 4

1. This illustration later appeared in C. R. Swindoll's timely book *Make Up Your Own Mind . . . About the Issues of Life* (Portland, Ore.: Multnomah, 1981), pp. 66–67. See also Charles A. Goodrum's *Treasures of the Library of Congress* (New York: Harry H. Abrams, 1980), p. 280.

2. See the author's *Keys to Spiritual Growth* (Chicago: Moody, 1983), pp. 11–21.

3. Boaz was not spoken of as an Ephrathite (cf. 1:2). He was not a part of the wealthy aristocracy.

4. Watson, p. 390.

5. This sentence, beginning with *halô' šāma'at bittî*, "do you not hear, my daughter," is interrogative in nature and expresses a *positive* wish. The

bittî, "my daughter," was regarded by many commentators as giving evidence of the disparity between their ages. The word really means "young lady," and there is no significant reason to believe that Boaz was more than ten years older than Ruth.

6. The addition of the word *gam,* "also," which seems superfluous, preserves a quaint, archaic manner of speech, and gives tacit proof of the fact that, as Morris has observed, "It does not seem as though the main facts recorded have to do with the remote past" (p. 239).

7. The expressions "do not leave . . . you shall stay . . ." are emphatic. The former uses *lō'* instead of the more common *'al,* and the latter employs an unusual preposition, *'im,* after "you shall stay." See also 1:14; 2:21, 23. It seems to give evidence of Boaz's special way of speaking. Kennedy says, "Of the seven examples of this archaism, four are in Ruth, (ii. 8, 21, iii. 4, 18), suggesting that the author of this book wished to give an archaic colour to this *(viz,* Boaz's) style, *to suit the period of the story*" (p. 31, italics added). With this last statement we cannot agree.

8. This sentence lacks a verb and has been variously translated "Keep your eyes on the field" or with emphasis on "and you shall *go,*" rendering the Hebrew, "Keeping your eyes on the field, go out after them. . . ." The latter translation ignores the *waw,* "and," and forces an unnatural construction upon the sentence.

9. The verb *yiqṣōrûn,* "they shall harvest," is masculine, whereas "after them" uses a feminine plural suffix. This would seem to imply that both men and women were involved in harvesting. It is possible that the men cut the crop and the women tied the stalks into bundles. Joüon, *Ruth* (p. 53), disagreed with this and believed that the feminine form was a textual error. He is hard pressed to maintain his theory, for the feminine form also occurs in 2:8, 9, 22, 23, and 3:2.

10. "And you shall go . . ." is here equivalent to an imperative.

11. "Have I not ordered the young men not to touch you," *halô' ṣiwwîtî 'et-hanne'ārîm lebiltî nog'ēk,* has caused many commentators to debate the meaning of *nāga',* "to molest." Sasson (p. 50) does not believe Ruth ran any risk of being sexually assaulted. See *TWOT,* 2:551; BDB, p. 619. Morris wrote, "One can imagine that the enthusiasm of the gleaners would cause them to encroach on the legitimate property of the owners of the crops unless they were checked, and that accordingly the reapers might repulse, by force, if necessary, any who came too near before the owners were through. Ruth would know this and keep her distance. Boaz's instruction to Ruth enabled her to work close to the reapers in a position specially favorable for gleaning. But this very position exposed her to the possibility of rude jests and even mishandling from the workmen. He now tells her that he has guarded against this by giving instructions to the reapers that they were to leave her

alone. His order would allow her to approach before other gleaners and thus ensure that she obtained a good reward for her labors, and this without being treated disrespectfully" (p. 275). Against these views is the use of *lebiltî* (see 1:13 and 3:10), implying a strong prohibition against anything that might lead to Ruth's being molested.

12. Harvesting is thirsty work. Joüon, *Ruth* (pp. 53f.), believed the content of these skins was wine. The verb "have drawn," however, as Campbell has noted, "is used exclusively for drawing water" (p. 98)—probably from the well of Bethlehem from which David, years later, wished to drink (2 Sam. 23:15, 16).

13. *Hithpa'el*, "she prostrated herself."

14. *Lehakîrēnî we'ānōkî nokriyyāh*, "that you should notice me, and I a stranger," employs the *Hiph'il* infinitive construct with the meaning of "to observe (with a view to recognition)"; *we'ānōkî*, "and I," according to Myers (pp. 19ff.), is further evidence of the early date of Ruth, for otherwise the shorter *'anî* would have been used; and finally, *nokriyyāh*, with the preceding pronominal suffix, forms a circumstantial noun clause.

15. The word *fully* stands at the beginning of the sentence indicating, by means of the word order, the emphasis designed by the writer. *Huggēd, huggad*, are *Hoph'als* of *ngd*, and, as Campbell reminds us, are a "mark of classical Hebrew prose" (p. 99).

16. Hebrew, "yesterday and the third day." See Morris, p. 276.

17. *Yešallēm YHWH po'olēk*, "may *Yahweh* repay your work," is unusual for there is no preposition or mark of the accusative. The use of *po'olēk*, "deeds, work, actions," was often found in Hebrew poetry, and always in the early period of Israel's literary history.

18. The reference to Yahweh's "wings," *kenāpāyw*, recalls Deuteronomy 32:27–38. "The metaphor," says Fuller, "is borrowed from a hen, which, with her clucking, summons together her straggling chickens, and then outstretcheth the fan of her wings to cover them" (pp. 139–40).

19. The use of the imperfect expresses a wish, "may I find."

20. Morison said, "To be one of [Boaz's] maidens was, in her estimation, to be a most desirable condition. She could not aspire to that. But as he had spoken so graciously to her heart, and soothed its sorrows, she trusted he would still befriend her" (p. 37). Boaz has done all this for her even though she is not one of his maids.

21. Morris, p. 277.

22. G. C. Morgan, *Living Messages of the Books of the Bible*, pp. 134–36.

23. Some translators (Luther, Coverdale, KJV) took the words "at meal-time" to be a part of what Boaz said to Ruth: "And Boaz said, 'At mealtime come here, and you shall eat.'" The punctuation of the MT seems to favor the translation we have adopted. Joüon, *Ruth* (pp. 57–

58), observed that the dramatic effect of Ruth's words (v. 13) would be utterly lost if Boaz's immediate reply to her was that she concerned herself with the mundane matter of food. This need not be so, for Boaz's invitation was further evidence of his concern.

24. W. M. Thompson in *The Land and the Book* (Grand Rapids: Baker, 1966) says, "A quantity of the best ears, not too ripe, are plucked with the stalks attached. These are tied into small parcels, a blazing fire is kindled with dry grass and thorn bushes, and the cornheads are held in it until the chaff is mostly burned off. The grain is thus sufficiently roasted to be eaten, and it is a favorite article all over the country" (p. 648).

    The *ḥōmeṣ*, "vinegar," (sometimes a liquid and sometimes a thin paste) could be either fresh or fermented (cf. Num. 6:3). In Psalm 69:21 it is the term used for the kind of drink a thirsty man would not want.

    When Boaz invites Ruth to sit "beside" (*miṣṣad*) his workers (i.e., within the circle), he is demonstrating a dramatic way that she is to be accepted as one of the group. When he himself serves her, he is showing that, in his eyes, she is worthy of such honor.

25. "And he reached to her" *wayyiṣboṭ-lāh*, occurs only here. The verb was thought to be derived from the Akkadian, *ṣābātu*. It bears a similarity to *ṣebāṭîm* (2:16) and, according to some philologists, was an eastern Semitism that found its way into early Hebrew usage.

    The three verbs, *wattōʼkal, wattiśbaʻ, wattōtar*, "and she ate, and was satisfied, and had some left over," are linked by three *waw* consecutives. They emphasize Boaz's generosity.

26. "Roasted grain," *qālî*, was a staple in the diet of the poorer people. See *TWOT*, 2:798–99.

27. "The Masoretes noted that this is one of some 80 instances where pathach remains without the pausal lengthening 'at the end of a verse'" (Kennedy, p. 37).

28. The jussive here conveyed the idea of "Let her glean (even between the sheaves)."

29. The *hiphʻil* imperfect, *taklîmûhā*, "shame, humiliate, disgrace," has caused commentators difficulty. In *The Land and the Book*, Thompson stated he had observed the kind of behavior that characterized the harvesting process, and that verbal abuse was the least of the offenses (p. 648). Campbell said that the use of this word "underscores Boaz's determination to protect Ruth from improper advances from the men" (p. 103). The fact that Boaz gave instruction personally to *all* his men, and did not content himself with an order to his overseer, seems to imply something serious. Sasson (p. 56) and Joüon, *Ruth* (pp. 60–61), felt the import of the words was too strong and preferred to amend the text (changing the root from *klm* to *klʼ*).

30. *Biblical Researches* (1841), 2:394.

Chapter 5

1. Mortimer Adler, *Six Great Ideas* (New York: Macmillan, 1981), p. 3.
2. James White, the London financier, had all that money could buy—material comforts, social position, power—and yet he had not found happiness. Ultimately he took his own life and, in a letter he left behind, said: "Gone are the nicer feelings and contentment. One day follows another with similar monotony. Life is just one drab day after another."
3. deVaux, pp. 39–40; see also F. C. Fensham, "Widow, Orphan, and the Poor in Ancient Eastern Legal and Wisdom Literature," *JNES* 21 (1962), pp. 129–39; *TDOT*, 1:287–91.
4. The plural form appears in the text.
5. There is some confusion over whether these words should be translated "her mother-in-law saw" or "she showed her mother-in-law." Translators line up on both sides. Perhaps the only decisive evidence is the absence of '*eṭ* before mother-in-law. This would seem to favor the translation we have adopted.
6. Literally, "from her satiety." This reveals both her hunger and Boaz's liberality.
7. Sasson (p. 58) treated '*ēypōh liqqaṭ hayyôm we'ānāh 'āśît* as two different questions. He was influenced by Joüon, *Ruth*, (p. 63), who considers the text to be faulty. Campbell pointed out that the text is to be regarded as synonymous parallelism "although the text as we have it connects the two questions with the conjunction 'and'" (p. 105). The '*ēypōh* and '*ānāh*, both asking the question "where," are much less frequent than '*ayyēh* (though, as BDB pointed out, '*ayyēh* was never used with verbs).
8. The "power to bless" versus the "power to curse" is something that should not pass unnoticed. The power to bless is essentially a characteristic of the Judeo-Christian religion. The power to curse is essentially pagan and was used when someone wanted to gain control over another. Its modern counterpart may be seen in threats, different forms of coercion, and malevolent manipulative devices. By way of contrast, invoking blessing on another leaves the individual free to respond to God's leading without feeling under obligation to the blesser.
9. Cox, p. 97.
10. Commentators have picked up on the supposed redundancy in "with whom she worked" and "with whom I worked." Some even pointed out that the LXX preserved the essence of Ruth's reply, but without the belabored repetition. When we bear in mind (1) that we are moving from indirect to direct discourse, (2) that in identifying the owner of the field it was necessary for Ruth to introduce him by referring back to Naomi's question, and (3) that in the recounting of the story the repeti-

tion added emphasis and also delayed the mention of the name of Boaz (thus increasing the suspense), the effect gained fully justified the process.

11. Campbell, p. 106.
12. "Living" (referring to Naomi and Ruth) is masculine plural. We would have expected a feminine plural. Inasmuch as the reference is to the *two* women, the situation is similar to the one in Ruth 1, where we suggested that this may be an early form of "corporate" address.
13. See Morris, p. 280. Cox (p. 98) is in essential agreement with this. Glueck, *Hesed in the Bible* (pp. 35ff.), believed that the clause modifies Boaz. Campbell said, "It is true that Boaz has done acts of *hesed* in chapter 2 and will yet do more, but the much more likely antecedent is Yahweh" (p. 106; cf. Gen. 24:27).
14. Cox, pp. 98–99.
15. For the fullest explanation see Leggett, pp. 73–139 and 181–201; see also A. R. Johnson, "The Primary Meaning of *G'L,*" *Studentenalmanak Vrije Universiteit* 1 (1953), pp. 71ff.
16. D. Daube, *Studies in Biblical Law* (New York: Ktav, 1947), pp. 44ff. Leggett cited the work of the Dutch theologian R. Sikkema, *De Lening in het Oude Testament* (1957), pp. 95–111, a work that was not available to this author.
17. I. Mendelsohn, "Slavery in the Ancient Near East," *BA* 9 (1946), 74–88; H. L. Ellison, "The Hebrew Slave," *EQ* 45 (1973), pp. 30–35; Morris, pp. 282–83.
18. M. Buttenweiser, "Blood Revenge and Burial Rites in Ancient Israel," *JAOS* 38–39 (1918), pp. 306ff.; J. Porter, "Legal Aspects of Corporate Personality," *VT* 15 (1968), pp. 365ff.
19. G. A. Cooke, *The Book of Ruth*, pp. 3–4; J. Mittleman, *Der altisraelitische Levirat* (Leiden: Ginsberg, 1934), p. 18; L. Epstein, *Marriage Laws in the Bible and the Talmud* (1942), pp. 85ff.
20. See Leggett, pp. 181–88.
21. Ruth still is referred to as a Moabitess. Many commentators pointed out that such repetition is unnecessary. See J. deWaard and E. A. Nida, *Translation of the Book of Ruth* (New York: United Bible Societies, 1973), p. 43. Others made a rather clumsy apology for it. Campbell (p. 107) remarked, "If it is redundant to have 'the Moabitess' expressed, it is equally redundant to repeat 'to her mother-in-law.'" The solution to this persistent, purposeful repetition must be found in the author's intent and theme. Ruth has no claim to the *gō'ēl* rites of Israel. Naomi has no right to expect her daughter-in-law to support her. By God's grace alone, Boaz will act according to the spirit of the Law and contract a *ge'ullah* marriage with Ruth, who will engage in such a marriage for the sake of Naomi.

22. The reference to *hanne'ārîm*, "young men," has led some to conclude that Ruth's libidinal drives were leading her away from her commitment to Naomi, and she was indeed thinking that marriage to one of them might be a means of escape from her present problems. Morris (p. 281), however, offered the suggestion that this term included *all* those engaged in the harvest, men as well as women. In verse 22 Naomi uses *na'arôtāyw*, "young women," (see v. 8) and this strengthens the view that *hanne'ārîm* refers to both sexes.

23. The use of *yipge'û-bāk*, "attack, fall upon," has been subject to a variety of interpretations. In Joshua 2:16, 1 Samuel 22:17–18, and 1 Kings 2:25–46 the word appears in its normal usage of "to strike down, to attack violently." While it is true that the context frequently determines the meaning, there is no indication here that Ruth's personal safety was not an issue. Morris (pp. 281–82) and Sasson (p. 62) did not believe that Ruth ran any risk. Campbell, however, said, "Naomi's instructions do appear to place more emphasis on Ruth's personal safety, although no other use of the word in the OT suggests sexual assault. Nevertheless, by this slight change of verb, from *ng'* to *pg'*, the storyteller may be nudging his audience along to think about the protection of the 'elect' women" (p. 108).

24. The reconstruction of the calendar of the ancient Hebrews has been made possible by the discovery of the Gezer Calendar (c. 925 B.C.). According to Deuteronomy 16:9–12 it seems evident that the time from the beginning of the barley harvest to the end of the wheat harvest was normally seven weeks, culminating in the Feast of Pentecost. W. F. Albright, in *Ancient Near Eastern Texts* (p. 320), and in an article in the *BASOR* 92 (Dec. 1943), pp. 25ff., and G. E. Wright, in *Biblical Archaeology* (Philadelphia: Westminster, 1962), pp. 183ff., showed that the precise time of the beginning of the harvest differed. The grain on the higher elevations ripened sooner than the grain on the lower elevations. In addition, there would also be a slight difference in the ripening of grain from south to north. The general time of harvest, however, ran from late April to early June.

25. Cox, pp. 99–100.

Chapter 6

1. *Conceptions of Modern Psychiatry* (New York: W. W. Norton, 1940), pp. 42–43.
2. Leggett, pp. 55, 58.
3. "Have I not been seeking . . ." and "is not Boaz our relative . . ." are illustrations of the Hebraic way of using the "abstract for the concrete,"

(i.e., of stating something in a positive way). See Wright, p. 40. The imperfect form of the first verb implies an active, continuous effort on Naomi's part.

Campbell (p. 116) drew attention to this negative form of rhetorical question with the addition of "daughter," and, linking it with 2:8–9 and 3:10, concluded that, because they spoke the same way, Naomi and Boaz were of the same age. Such a conclusion bears consideration. Campbell, however, overlooked certain facts, namely, (1) the use of the word "daughter" in situations where a social superior is addressing a social subordinate; (2) the use of the perfect tense of the verb in 2:8–9, whereas in 3:1 we have the imperfect; and (3) the possibility that such an expression could easily be a form of provincialism without having any bearing on one's age. These issues need to be considered before any decision is reached regarding Boaz's age.

4. The word here is *mānôaḥ*, a cognate of *menûḥâ* (1:9). It implied, passively, the "rest" a woman entered when she was spared all the nagging insecurities of life; and actively, the security and benefits that occured to a woman who entered marriage. The meaning was reinforced by Naomi's "that it may be well with you."

5. The use of *mōda'tānû*, "our kindred," has posed problems for interpreters. The word comes from the root *yd'*, "to know." It appears in the text as a feminine noun, and the suffix *-ānû* (instead of the expected *-ēnû)* is analymous. Its meaning is clear; Campbell (pp. 117f.) discussed the grammatical and syntactical problems.

6. The meaning of *gōren*, "threshing floor," has been the subject of considerable debate. The structure of the sentence, *hinnēh-hû' zōreh 'et-gōren haśśe'ōrîm hallāyelāh*, "he is the one who winnows the threshing floor of barley," has led many to question the accuracy of the text. Ruth 2:23 mentions the wheat harvest following the barley harvest. Why then had the grain not been winnowed at the time of harvesting? Assuming the correctness of the text, where had the grain been kept? And where was the threshing floor?

In answer to the first question, it is possible that the harvested bundles of barley were brought either into the city or kept in some form of shelter until the time of winnowing. Such structures, if not in the city, would probably have been near the threshing floor, and, from what we can deduce from the history of the times, must have been closely guarded. If the reapers harvested the wheat immediately after the barley, there is no reason to doubt the accuracy of the text, which identified the activity here as involving the winnowing of barley. Joüon, *Ruth*, tried to escape the difficulty by regarding the clause as metonymic, "the product of the threshing floor" (p. 67). His reasoning was inconclusive.

Second, Campbell (pp. 117–19) discussed the location of the threshing floor at length. He proposed changing the text from *šeʿōrîm*, "barley," to *šeʿarîm*, "gates" (ignoring the difficulty of whether the barley
was winnowed ahead of the wheat), and, on the basis of a passage like 1
Kings 22:10, places the activity of the evening close to the gate of
Bethlehem. His evidence for such a practice being done in or near the
gates of other cities is impressive. In the context of Ruth 3, however,
Naomi's *weyāradty*, "go down," would seem to imply a place other than
in or near the gate of the city, for the gates of cities were normally
situated on high ground (cf. 4:1).

7. The importance of *hallāyelāh*, "tonight," or "this very night," adds a
   sense of urgency to Naomi's words. Her plan, conceived some six
   weeks previously (2:20), and carefully worked out, now needed immediate execution.

   The use of *laylāh*, "night," is not the same as *ʿereb*, "evening" (2:17).
   Joüon, *Ruth* (p. 67), developed a case for regarding the "night" as being
   any part of the afternoon (cf. Josh. 2:2ff.). Morris, whose judgment is
   usually balanced and discriminating, said, "It is possible that the wind
   in the daytime was very strong or very gusty, which would make winnowing difficult. If these were the conditions, then work at night might
   well be preferable. L. P. Stone said that in the summer the wind blows
   from about four or five o'clock until a little after sunset" (p. 285).

   Although not wishing to appear to contradict so worthy a commentator, the author observed, on a visit to the Holy Land, modern Israeli
   farmers in the higher elevations and South of the Horns of Hattin
   winnowing grain at midday. See D. Baly, *Geography of the Bible* (New
   York: Harper & Row, 1974), pp. 46, 64.

8. Joüon, *Ruth* stated that "Ruth was to bathe and anoint herself with
   aromatic oil" (p. 68). He referred to the apocryphal book of Judith
   (10:3) for support. Campbell (p. 120) referred to the Septuagint and the
   Lucianic manuscripts, which specify that she was to rub herself with
   myrrh. Biblical evidence for "anointing oneself" may be found in Esther
   2:12; Psalm 45:8; Proverbs 7:17; and particularly in the Song of Solomon
   1:3, 13; 4:14; 5:1, 5, 13.

9. Some take *śimlāh*, "garment," to imply that Ruth had only one piece of
   clothing (cf., Joüon, *Ruth*, p. 69). Others believed that she "put off her
   'widow's weeds'" (e.g., Watson, p. 401). However, if Ruth had character-
   istically worn clothes that would identify her as a widow, Boaz would
   not have asked to whom she belonged in 2:5. Because Ruth later was
   found to possess a *miṭpaḥat*, "cloak, shawl, covering," she may have
   possessed another dress (used on this occasion) that the Hebrew text
   had not alluded to heretofore (cf. 4:3, where Naomi had land not previously brought to the attention of the reader).

10. *Weyāraḏty*, "go down," should present no problem to the interpreter. Bethlehem was situated on a ridge jutting out from the mountain chain. It would be natural for people leaving the city to "go down" into the valley, unless they were going to Jerusalem six miles away; then the expression would be to "go up." Some writers, however, in an endeavor to link what takes place in this chapter with the sexual orgies associated with fertility rites, claim that Ruth "went up" to the high place to participate in these pagan activities. Cf. H. G. May, "Ruth's Visit to the High Place in Bethlehem," *JRAS* 75 (1939), pp. 75–78; W. E. Staples, "The Book of Ruth," *AJSL* 53 (1937), pp. 155-57.

11. The use of *tiwwāḏeʾî*, "to be known," is regarded by some as evidence that Naomi's plan involved sexual relations between Ruth and Boaz. Although the verb *yāḏaʿ* is used of "carnal knowledge," we must remember that *niphʿal* never conveys this idea, whereas the *qal* may (depending on the context). See G. Coats, "Widows' Rights: A Crux in the Structure of Genesis 38," *CBQ* 34 (1972), pp. 464ff.; S. Sherman and J. Curtis, "Divine Human Conflicts in the Old Testament," *JNES* 28 (1969), pp. 234–37; cf. J. Gray, *Joshua, Judges, Ruth* (1967), p. 417.

12. The precise meaning of *wegillit margelōṭāyw*, "and uncover his 'feet,'" has received extensive comment from Campbell, (p. 121), Joüon, *Ruth* (p. 69), and Sasson, (pp. 69–71). E. Robertson, "The Plot of the Book of Ruth," *BJRL* 32 (1950), pp. 225, 228, portrayed Naomi as a scheming, pragmatic woman who "outwitted" Boaz who, following the night on the threshing floor, found himself in a compromised position and was compelled to marry Ruth.

13. F. C. Fensham, "Widow, Orphan and the Poor in Ancient Near Eastern Legal and Wisdom Literature," *JNES* 21 (1962), pp. 129–39.

14. M. Weinfeld, "Ruth," *Encyclopedia Judaica* (New York: Macmillan, 1971), p. 520.

15. Morris, p. 287.

16. The use of *wattaʿaś kekōl* is taken by most scholars to mean "she did everything exactly" as her mother-in-law commanded her.

17. Campbell (p. 121) stated that Ruth did exactly what Naomi told her to do—up to a point. Then, where Naomi had said, "He will tell you what to do," Ruth instead graciously and with befitting courtesy suggests what he is to do. In this we see her desire to look out for Naomi's interests.

18. Harvest time was a time for feasting and enjoyment (cf. Isa. 9:3).

19. Sasson (p. 73) said that in Hebrew we frequently encounter *lēb*, "heart," used with a form of the root *ṭōb* or *yṭb*, "to be good," to describe various forms of emotional well-being (cf. 1 Kings 8:66; Prov. 15:15; Eccles. 9:7); Robinson, 1:50; 2:35, 83, 306ff.

20. See Joüon, *Ruth*, pp. 70–71.

21. For comments on the usage of *ballāṭ*, "quietly, secretly," see Joüon, *Ruth*, p. 71; Myers, p. 28; and the Hebrew text of Judges 4:21; 1 Samuel 24:5.

22. Confusion exists over the meaning of *wategal margelōṭāyw*, "uncover his feet." In 3:7 it specified what Ruth uncovered. In 3:8 and 14 it specified where Ruth slept. In some other passages of Scripture the phrase refers to the sexual organs of either men or women (cf. Judg. 3:24; 1 Sam. 24:3; 2 Kings 18:27 [Isa. 36:12]; Isa. 7:20; Ezek. 16:25). From the context it appears as if Boaz's feet are intended. See Cooke, p. 10; and C. Lattey, *The Book of Ruth* (London: Longmans, Green, 1935), pp.15–16.

23. The Hebrew is most expressive: "in the half of the night . . ." Boaz awakened, probably due to the cold, and when groping for the portion of his cloak that covered his feet discovered a woman there.

24. The use of *wayyeḥerad*, "shuddered, trembled," may have been on account of sudden fear or as a result of the cold. See Joüon, *Ruth*, pp. 71–72. (See also footnote 26 below.)

25. The Hebrew contains the feminine singular *'at*. Apparently there was sufficient light from the moon for Boaz to be able to vaguely discern a woman's form without being able to pick out any recognizable features.

26. Commenting on Boaz's "who are you?", Sasson (pp. 76–78) conjectured that his superstitious nature caused him to fear the presence of the female demon *Lilith*. It would appear as if Sasson read too much from pagan sources into the text of Ruth.

27. The word used here is *'āmāh*, "handmaid," and differs slightly from *šiphāh*, "maid-servant" (2:13), though the exact distinction between these two words is very slight. See A. Jepsen, "*Amah* and *Schiphciah*," *VT* 8 (1958), pp. 293–97; Morris, p. 289.

28. The use of *kenāpekā*, "wing," may refer back to 2:12. Some commentators, however, believe that the word refers to Boaz's "skirt" or the border of his cloak. The symbolism was the same regardless of whether *kenāpekā* is "wing" or "cloak." See *Theologisches Handwörterbuch zum Alten Testament*, ed. E. Jenni and C. Westermann (Stuttgart: Verlag W. Kohlammer, 1971), 1:835. The issue revolves around whether *kenāpekā* is singular or a plural written defectively. The MT is singular and reference to Deuteronomy 22:30 (Heb., v. 31); 27:20; and Ezekiel 16:8 seems to verify the assumption that the singular is correct.

29. The expression *kî gō'ēl 'attāh*, "for you [are] a redeemer," is significant. The article is absent. Ruth was either being very modest in her form of address (not wishing to press her claim too hard), or she was aware that there was a *gō'ēl* nearer of kin to Elimelech than Boaz.

30. We observe again the frequency with which the pious people of the story invoke the blessing of the Lord on others. This is truly remark-

able and stands in stark contrast to pagan belief and practice. See C. J. Barber and J. D. Carter, *Always a Winner* (Ventura, Calif.: Gospel Light, 1977), pp. 59–71.

31. Morris said: "The kindness *at the beginning* (KJV, RV) will be that which Ruth showed to Naomi in not forsaking her and in gleaning to provide for her needs. Now to this she adds a further evidence of her regard for family relationships. She has not followed natural inclinations (in seeking a young man in marriage), but has shown a responsible attitude to the family in looking to her *gō'ēl* as her marriage partner" (p. 290). It could also refer to Ruth's initial decision when she turned from her parents and homeland and chose to look after her mother-in-law. See Sasson, p. 84; Joüon, *Ruth*, p. 74.

32. The article is used with *baḥûrîm*, "the [choice] young men"—those who are handsome and in the prime of life. It stands in contrast to *ne'arîm*, "youths," and *zeqēnîm*, "old men." Morris offered the following pertinent comment: "Boaz sees her faithfulness in the fact that when she thought of marriage Ruth did not go after *young men* . . . whether poor or rich. She preferred to keep to family connections and thus showed her respect for the right. She did not simply let her own personal inclinations rule her. . . . There is an article with *young men.* It is not 'young men' in general that is meant but 'the young men,' the definite group of young men in the village. We should not overlook the implied compliment to Ruth. Boaz clearly was certain that had she wished Ruth might have married a rich young man. There would be no point in praising her faithfulness to family obligations otherwise" (p. 290).

33. The question again arises, How old was Boaz at the time of these events? We have before suggested that he was in his mid-thirties, older than Ruth yet younger than Elimelech would have been had he still been alive. To avoid having Boaz married to two women at once, the *Talmud* (Baba Bathra, 91a) had his wife die most opportunely, at a time coinciding with Ruth's arrival in Bethlehem. We mention this to show how myths have developed around the person of Boaz. The *Midrash* (Ruth Rabba, III:10) depicted Boaz as an octogenarian. Rabbinic literature also saw Boaz dying as soon as Ruth had conceived (*Talmud*, Yalq. Shim'oni, 608). Morris (pp. 290–91) and Rowley, "The Marriage of Ruth," *HTR* 40 (1947), pp. 78ff., believed him to be much older than Ruth. However, few men lived beyond their mid-forties in those times (though affluence did tend to prolong life), and when Boaz referred to Ruth as "my daughter," it did not mean that he was old enough to be her father.

34. The importance of "the gate" in the city life is attested by passages of Scripture such as Deuteronomy 5:14; 12:12; 14:21, 27–29; 15:7; 16:11, 14,

18; 17:2, 5, 8; 18:6; 23:16 (Heb., v. 17); 24:14; 26:12. See Campbell (p. 124); Morris (p. 291); W. M. Thompson, *Southern Palestine and Jerusalem* (London: T. Nelson, 1880), pp. 29–30.

35. The Hebrew *'ēšet ḥayil*, "a woman of valor," is the same expression used to describe Boaz in 2:1, *'îš gibbôr ḥayil*, "a mighty man of valor," (except that in the case of Boaz, there is the addition of *gibbôr*, "mighty"). Our preference in translating 2:1 was to see Boaz as a man of valor rather than riches, because here, where the same word is used of Ruth, we know that she was in extreme poverty. The emphasis in both instances is on the quality of the person rather than on his or her possessions. See Campbell (p. 125), Joüon, *Ruth* (p. 74), Morris (p. 291), and Sasson (pp. 87–88) for differing viewpoints.

36. *We'attāh kî 'omnām kî 'im gō'ēl 'ānôkî*, "and now [it is] true that I [am] a redeemer," presents difficulties to the translator on account of the numerous particles and adverbs and the absence of verbs. Certain scholars (Campbell, p. 125; Myers, p. 25; Joüon, *Ruth*, pp. 74–75) deleted certain words or amended the text. W. Staples, "Notes on Ruth 2, 20 and 3, 12," *AJSL* 54 (1937–38), p. 62, takes the *'m* to be a negative and regards Boaz's statement as a disclaimer: "But now, as a matter of fact, I am really *not* [your] *gō'ēl*." This view is contradicted by the evidence in Ruth 4.

37. See Watson, pp. 398, 402.

38. For a discussion of *lînî hallaylāh*, "stay tonight," and why certain letters have been printed in larger type, see Campbell (p. 125), and Sasson (pp. 88–89).

39. Morris (p. 203) drew attention to the fact that Boaz does not use the word *marry* when speaking of the other kinsman's rights. Boaz addressed himself rather to the responsibilities of a *gō'ēl*. However, his *I* (in "I will redeem you") was emphatic.

40. Campbell (p. 126) pointed out that the terminology here differs from the vocabulary of Deuteronomy 25:5–10. He conjectured that this is because Boaz knew that his contemplated action did not conform exactly to the Mosaic statute but only adhered to its general intent. Boaz, however, may also have been quoting Deuteronomy 25 from memory.

41. The phrase *ḥay YHWH*, "as Yahweh lives," appears to be a standard form of oath. See G. Gerleman, *Theologisches Handwörterbuch zum Alten Testament*, 1:554–55.

42. Quoted in Morris, p. 287.

43. Watson, p. 398.

44. Taylor, p. 77.

45. Sasson, p. 81; E. Neufeld, *Ancient Hebrew Marriage Laws*, pp. 31ff.; cf., *Talmud*, Baba Bathra, 91a.

46. See P. R. Ackerman and M. M. Kappelman, *Signals* (New York: Dial Press, 1978); M. Strommen, ed., *Five Cries of Youth* (New York: Harper &

Row, 1974); and C. J. Barber and G. H. Strauss, *The Effective Parent* (San Bernardino, Calif.: Here's Life, 1980), for discussions of how parents may become more sensitive to their children's silent pleas.

47. C. J. Barber and A. A. Barber, *Your Marriage Has Real Possibilities* (San Bernardino, Calif.: Here's Life, 1981), pp. 1–11.

48. N. O'Neill and G. O'Neill, *Open Marriage* (New York: M. Evans, 1973).

49. *Saturday Review* 53 (March 1970), p. 23.

Chapter 7

1. *Harper's Magazine* 56 (Jan. 1976), pp. 75–78.

2. Morison observed: "The anonymous relative does not conceal the idea that it would be only on the ground of doing what would be *for his own interest* that he could entertain for consideration the proposal of Naomi. He likewise assumed that if Boaz would be willing to act the kinsman's part, it would be simply because it could be turned to account *for his own interest.* He did not know that there was in Boaz's heart a love that truly 'seeketh not her own,' but in honor prefers the things of another" (p. 62).

3. The word translated "lay at his feet," *margelōtāw*, has been written defectively. We would have expected the addition of a *yôd* between the last two consonants. The importance of Ruth's action was that she took the same position as in verse 8. She did not cuddle up beside Boaz.

4. The Hebrew *wattāqom* is feminine, "and she arose." Joüon, *Ruth* (p. 77), proposed to change the text to read *wayyāqom*, "and he arose," to fit the statement that follows: "And Boaz said. . . ." Rudolph (p. 46) suggested the addition of *bidbārō*, "at his request," believing that this word has been lost. After due consideration of these proposals, we see no real reason for not following the biblical text.

5. The phrase *yaqqîr 'îš 'et-rē'ēhû*, "a man could recognize his neighbor," refers to that period of time preceding dawn when it is still too dark for one to discern any recognizable features. All that may be seen are shapes or silhouettes against the skyline. Morris (p. 203) drew our attention to a reference in the *Mishnah* (Yebamoth 2:8, Danby's translation, p. 220) in which a man was prevented from performing a levirate marriage if it was suspected that he had sexual relations with a slave or a Gentile woman.

6. The article *the* appears before the word "woman." Previously Boaz had spoken of Ruth as a *ne'ārāh*, "young woman," or in more affectionate, familial terms as a *bat*, "daughter." Neither of these is now appropriate. Both he and Ruth have committed themselves to each other, and he has pledged himself to marry her. The word *'iššāh*, "woman," may also

bear the meaning of "wife." The addition of the article would have been most appropriate, for Boaz had a specific person in mind.

7. Boaz's request for Ruth's cloak, *hābî hammiṭpaḥat 'ašer-'ālayik*, was peculiar. Joüon, *Grammaire* (#75k [pp. 150–51]), and Myers (p. 18) offer suggestions regarding its etymology. It would seem to be an imperitival form of the root *yhb*, "to give," (cf. Ps. 55:22 [Heb. v. 23]). Campbell (p. 127) discussed the usage of the word based on its occurrence in other passages. Joüon, *Ruth* (p. 78), omitted this phrase from his discussion and passed on to a consideration of the vocalization of *'eḥozî-bāh*, "and hold on to it." Boaz has Ruth assist him as he measures six *seāh* of barley into her mantle.

8. A problem arises as to how much barley Boaz gives Ruth. The Hebrew text, *wayyāmod šēš-še'ōrîm*, "and he measured six [measures] of barley," leaves out the quantity. D. J. Wiseman in "Weights and Measures," *IBD*, 3:1637–39, described the Hebrew "dry measures of capacity": *ḥōmer* or *kōr*, (220 liters); *ephah* (22 liters); *seāh* (7.3 liters); and *'ōmer* (2.4 liters). Although women in the Near East are used to carrying large loads, Boaz's gift could not have been either six *ḥōmers* or *ephahs*. We are therefore left with either the *seāh* or the *'ōmer*. Six *'ōmers* of barley would have been less than Ruth had gleaned after spending all day in the field (cf. 2:17), and this would have been a small gift to send to Naomi, particularly when the emphasis of the passage is on the sacrificial generosity of Boaz. Furthermore, *'ōmer* is masculine, whereas the adjective "six" is feminine. *Seāh*, however, is feminine and better suits the syntax. When it is noted that Boaz had to lift the load onto Ruth, it is evident that something heavier than an *'ōmer* was meant. Brockelmann, *Hebräische Syntax* (p. 77), listed passages in which an unspecified commodity (e.g., grain or oil) was used with only a numeral specifying amount. His classification of materials is helpful to the busy researcher even if some of his conclusions are misleading. For a fuller discussion see Campbell (p. 128), who proposed amending the text from *še'arîm* to *še'ōrîm*, an unknown and elsewhere unattested measure; see also Sasson (pp. 96–97), and deVaux, (pp. 200–203).

9. The purpose of Boaz's gift to Naomi has been variously explained: Paul Humbert, "Art et leçon de l'histoire de Ruth," *Révue de théologie et philosophie*, N.S. 26 (1938), pp. 257–86, proposed that this would give Ruth an excuse for her visit to the threshing floor. (He overlooked the fact that anyone seeing Ruth with such an accumulation of barley would think that she had come by it illegally.) Gunkel, *Ruth* (pp. 78f.), suggested that the barley was a symbolic gift assuring Naomi of Boaz's honorable intentions where Ruth was concerned; Rudolph (p. 57) believed that the gift to Naomi was repayment for her thoughtfulness

toward him in choosing him as her (and Ruth's) redeemer; Staples, "The Book of Ruth," *AJSL* 53 (1937), p. 57, advanced the untenable theory that the six measures of barley are a gift to the grain god; May, in "Ruth's Visit to the High Place at Bethlehem," *JRAS* (1939), p. 78, regarded Boaz's present to Ruth as payment for sexual favors. (He treats this in the same light as Judah's gift to Tamar, Gen. 38; cf. Hos. 9:1). Rowley, "The Marriage of Ruth," *HTR* XL (1947), pp. 87–88, rebutted these false hypotheses.

The *Midrash* (Ruth Rabbah, VII, 2) advances the equally improbable theory that six *seāhs* of barley is the minimum *mōhar*, or dowry, given to the parents of the bride. This is most unlikely; in passages like Leviticus 27:4–7, the minimum worth of a woman is set at thirty shekels of silver, and six measures of barley would have fetched much less at the market. It seems preferable to see in this gift to Naomi a pledge on the part of Boaz to care for her and perform the responsibilities of a *gō'ēl.*.

10. Most commentators and translators amended the text to "she," changing *wayyābō' hā'îr*, "and he went to the city," to *wattābō' hā'îr*, "and she went to the city," (see Joüon, *Ruth*, p. 78; Morris, p. 295), claiming that "he" must be a scribal error. But we do not see why the MT should not be followed. Boaz went to the city, possibly to his house to obtain the necessary money; and Ruth returned to Naomi. Joüon's conjecture (p. 78) that Boaz was unlikely to have left the threshing floor overlooked the fact that there are other men there who would defend Boaz's harvest in the (unlikely) event of a raid (taking place so soon before dawn). The only problem to this view concerns the translation of 4:1. Does the verb look at the action as taking place (i.e., Boaz going up) or as Boaz already having gone to the city?

The circumstantial clause beginning with a *waw* conversive "then" followed by a perfect verb simply looks at the action that takes place, and does not indicate whether this is before, after, or contemporaneous with the events just described. See KD 4:487. For comments on the verb *'ālāh*, "went up," see Joüon, *Ruth* (pp. 79–80), Campbell (pp. 140–41), and Sasson (p. 104). The writer of Ruth purposely avoided using the imperfect (which would have been expected).

It should be noted that in 4:1 Boaz "went up to the gate" (not to the city as would be expected if he were leaving the threshing floor; cf. 3:15*b*). The impression left us is that he went up to the gate from his house, for city gates were invariably situated at higher elevations where cities were built on hillsides, and only at lower levels if more than one gate led into the city. The gate of the city where the court convened, to which Boaz went, would obviously have been the chief entrance into the city, situated on its imposing elevation.

11. Naomi's greeting, *mî-'at bittî*, which literally means, "Who are you, my daughter," has been the subject of endless discussion. Morris (p. 295) believed that Naomi could not recognize Ruth when she knocked on the door of their cottage, but saw only the figure of a woman. This would be plausible except for the addition of the words "my daughter" (cf. Boaz's question in 3:9, where *bittî* is omitted). Joüon, *Ruth* (p. 78), and Rudolph (p. 57) took the *mî* as an "accusative of condition." Gerleman (p. 34) took *mî* to be an interrogative particle with the meaning of "Is it you?" For a more extensive discussion see Sasson, pp. 100–1. We have chosen the tentative translation, "How did things go, my daughter," but realize the subjectivity of this choice.

12. See Campbell (p. 129) and Sasson (pp. 101–2) for the various views regarding the significance of this gift to Naomi.

13. Naomi's *'ēyk yippōl dābār* . . . and *kî-'im-killâ haddābār*, "how [the] matter falls" (i.e., turns out) . . . and "until he has completed the matter," (where *kî-'im* is used instead of *'ad 'ašer*), seem to denote a condition that must be fulfilled before the preceding statement can be brought to completion. Morris (p. 296n) noted that the first *dābār* ("matter") lacks the article, whereas the second ("the thing") has it.

14. See S. L. Greenslade, *The Cambridge History of the Bible* (Cambridge: Cambridge U., 1963) 3:166, and G. MacGregor, *A Literary History of the Bible* (Nashville: Abingdon, 1968), p. 211.

15. The emphasis in the text is on the quantity of barley. Ruth apparently intended to stress Boaz's generosity as she recounted to Naomi the events of the night.

16. For a treatment of the function of city gates and their importance in the life of the people, see W. M. Thompson, *The Land and the Book* (New York: Harper and Brothers, 1886), 1:27–32; Morris, p. 297.

17. The term *wehinnēh haggō'ēl 'ōbēr*, "and, behold, the kinsman passing by," draws attention to the immediacy of what happened. Campbell (p. 141) translated *wehinnēh*, "and just then."

18. The imperatives contain the cohortative *ā*. It was the writer's way of adding emphasis. He revealed through this kind of literary device how deftly Boaz took command of the situation. Campbell added, "Boaz acts with authority and at a determined pace" (p. 141).

I have omitted *pelōnî 'almōnî* from the translation because these Hebrew words virtually defy explanation. Some translate them "Such and such," or "So and so." Older writers believed they were the equivalent of "John Doe," or some expression given in place of a personal name. The effect was to indicate someone who, for whatever reason, should not or could not be named. For an explanation of the different ideas behind this expression, see Sasson, pp. 105–7.

19. Evidently there are "elders" present as well as others "sitting [in the gate]," and Boaz included the *yōšebîm*, "onlookers," out of courtesy. The emphasis came from the repetition of *neged*, "before." See deVaux, pp. 152–57.

20. Considerable discussion surrounds *mākerāh no'omî*, "Naomi has sold." The issue concerns the interpretation of the verb as well as the question of Naomi's right to sell land.

    Mākerāh is a perfect, feminine, third person singular verb. Wright (p. 55), KD (p. 488), and D. R. G. Beattie, "The Book of Ruth as Evidence for Israelite Legal Practice," *VT* 24 (1974), p. 1, translated this as describing action that has already taken place. S. R. Driver, *Treatise on the Use of the Tenses in Hebrew* (Oxford: Clarendon, 1881), said: "The perfect is employed to indicate actions, the accomplishment of which lies indeed in the future, but is regarded as dependent upon such an unalterable determination of the will that it may be spoken of as having actually taken place: thus a resolution, promise, or decree, especially a Divine one, is very frequently announced in the perfect tense. A striking instance is afforded by Ruth (iv. 3) when Boaz, speaking of Naomi's determination to sell her land, says . . . [*mākerāh no'omî*] literally, 'has sold' (has resolved to sell. The English idiom would be 'is selling')" (pp. 13–14). With this judgment A. B. Davidson, *Hebrew Syntax* (Edinburgh: T. & T. Clark, 1901), p. 41, is in essential agreement. The subsequent context (4:5, 9) indicated that the property had not been sold.

    The issue surrounding Naomi's possession of land is not so easily resolved; according to Numbers 27:8–11, the right to hold property passed through the male line. See J. Morgenstern, "The Book of the Covenant, Part II," *Hebrew Union College Annual* 7 (1930), p. 174; J. Weingreen, "The Case of the Daughters of Zelophehad," *VT* 16 (1966), p. 522; Z. Falk, *Hebrew Law in Bible Times* (Jerusalem: Wahrmann Books, 1964), p. 159; the extensive discussion by M. Burrows in "The Marriage of Boaz and Ruth," *JBL* 59 (1940), p. 448; K. H. Henrey, "Land Tenure in the Old Testament," *PEQ* 41 (1954), p. 9; and Leggett (pp. 211–22) alerted the reader to the complexity of the problem. Sasson (pp. 108–14) provided an evaluation of the various theories.

    In answer to Rowley's question as to where Naomi suddenly acquired land after coming back to Judah penniless (see *HTR* 40, p. 78), we offer the following explanation (also reached independently by Sasson): Elimelech and his family left Bethlehem at a time of severe famine. The fields were dry and perhaps had not been plowed in more than a year. Elimelech did not plan to stay in Moab very long and probably left his plot of land in the care of a relative or friend. This individual undoubtedly was given the right to cultivate the land and harvest the crop as soon as conditions became favorable.

Elimelech's stay in Moab was longer than expected. In fact, more than ten years passed before Naomi, Elimelech's widow, returned. It was the harvest season and Naomi could not lay claim to the land and sell it while it was being harvested. Now that the threshing was over, Naomi proceeded with her plans to sell the portion of the field that Elimelech had owned.

In the face of all the controversy over whether a widow can *legally* or *physically* own and sell land, the Book of Ruth seems to indicate that although the Mosaic law laid down the basic principles by which God's people were to be governed, it allowed considerable latitude (cf. 2 Kings 8:1–3, 6). The important point of the law was that the land remained in the family (or, if this failed, the tribe) and did not pass into the hands of outsiders should a widow remarry.

21. This expression furnishes us with a fine example of the picturesque meaning of *lē'mōr*, "I will open" or, as here, "uncover." The imagery is graphic and conjures up the idea of slightly moving the hair so as to divulge to the listener something of great importance.

22. There is a change of person here, as if Boaz, to keep the attention of those witnessing the proceedings, turned to them and said, "but if *he* will not redeem it." See Morison, p. 61; Morris, p. 303; and Sasson, p. 118.

23. The *I* is emphatic. It was as if Boaz knew that this unnamed relative was envious of his standing in the community and did not want anything to enhance his position. In emphasizing his willingness to redeem the land, Boaz said, in effect, "And I am right behind you" in order of kin. It seems as if the unnamed kinsman was glad to have the opportunity to add to his patrimonial possession the property that belonged to Elimelech. However, as soon as Boaz introduced Ruth as a separate appurtenance of Elimelech's estate, the kinsman's feelings changed. He remembered Boaz's statement "I am next in line after you" and availed himself of the means of escape from a difficult situation.

24. Verse 5 is permeated with perplexing interpretative problems. *Beyôm-qenôtekā haśśādeh*, "in the day of your acquiring [i.e., buying] the field" stresses the imminence of the act that the unnamed kinsman agreed to perform. *Beyôm* can also mean "at the time of" or "when." (See Joüon, *Grammaire*, #129 [p. 392]. See also deVaux [pp.180–81] for his discussion of time in the ancient Near East.)

There is no problem translating *qānāh*, "to buy, purchase." The difficulty comes in linking it with *ûmē'ēt*, "then from" (Ruth). To purchase land simultaneously from two people is easy to imagine. The difficulty comes later when the same word is used in connection with Ruth: *qānîtāy lehāqîm šēm-hammēt 'al-naḥalātô*, "you have 'bought' [her] to raise up the name of the dead on his inheritance." Does this verse imply that women were "bought" as brides? See Neufeld, *Ancient Hebrew Marriage Laws* (pp. 240ff.). D. H. Weiss, "The Use of *QNH* in Connection with Marriage," *HTR* 57 (1964), pp. 244–48, maintained that the verb *qnh* is only used in the Mishnah of marriage when other transactions are first involved (p. 246). See also M. Burrows, "Levirate Marriage in Israel," *JBL* 59 (1940), pp. 23–33. With these considerations in mind, and for the sake of consistency, we chose to translate *qānāh* as "acquire."

A further complication concerns the *mem* in *mē'ēt*, "to buy, purchase, acquire." Campbell (p. 146) regarded it as enclitic; Sasson (pp. 120ff.) rejected this, amended *qānîtā*, "you purchase, acquire," to *qānîtî*, "I purchase, acquire," and thereby believed he had solved the problem. For a further discussion of the issues see T. and D. Thompson, "Some Legal Problems in the Book of Ruth," *VT* 18 (1968), pp. 79–99; and L. M. Epstein, *Marriage Laws in the Bible and the Talmud* (1942), pp. 81, 85–86, 114, 122.

25. deVaux, pp. 21–22, 38.
26. The near kinsman's response, *lō' 'ûkal lig'āwl-î*, "I am not able to redeem for myself," is most interesting. He does not say that he *will* not redeem the land, but that he cannot. The reason he gives is "lest I ruin my own inheritance." Note the "I . . . my . . . own." Joüon, *Ruth* (p. 84), believed that he was exaggerating the condition in which he would find himself. Beattie (p. 262) believed that the *gō'ēl*'s words imply nothing more than "I cannot afford it." Cassel, *Ruth*, however, believed the man to be superstitious. "It must be her Moabitish nationality that forms the ground, such as it is, of the kinsman's refusal. Elimelech's misfortunes had been popularly ascribed to his emigration to Moab; the death of Chilion and Mahlon to their marriages with Moabitish women. This it was that had endangered their inheritance. The *goël* feared a similar fate. He thought that he ought not to take into his house a woman, marriage with whom has already been visited with the extinguishment of a family in Israel" (pp. 47–48). Most English commentators (who may have relied heavily on Lange's *Commentary* for their information) adhere to this view. See Cox, *Ruth*, pp. 138–40. In view of this kinsman's self-centeredness, it seems preferable to conclude that he did not want the responsibility of another wife and an addition to his family, with the sure knowledge that the portion of the field he was buying would in time pass out of his possession.
27. KD deals with the question of how Naomi came to possess Elimelech's property. They said, "So far as the fact itself was concerned, the field, which Naomi had sold from want, was the hereditary property of her deceased husband, and ought therefore to descend to her sons according to the standing rule of right; and in this respect, therefore, it was

Ruth's property quite as much as Naomi's. From the negotiation between Boaz and the nearer redeemer, it is very evident that Naomi had sold the field which was the hereditary property of her husband, and was lawfully entitled to sell it. But as landed property did not descend to wives according to the Israelitish law, but only to children, and when there were no children, to the nearest relatives of the husband (Num. xxvii. 8–11), when Elimelech died his field properly descended to his sons; and when they died without children, it ought to have passed to his nearest relations. Hence the question arises, what right had Naomi to sell her husband's field as her own property? The Rabbis suppose that the field had been presented to Naomi and Ruth by their husbands (*vid. Selden*, de success, in bona def. c. 15). But Elimelech could not lawfully give his hereditary property to his wife, as he left sons behind him when he died, and they were the lawful heirs; and Mahlon also had no more right than his father to make such a gift. There is still less foundation for the opinion that Naomi was an heiress, since even if this were the case, it would be altogether inapplicable to the present affair, where the property in question was not a field which Naomi had inherited from her father, but the field of Elimelech and his sons. The true explanation is no doubt the following: The law relating to the inheritance of the landed property of Israelites who died childless did not determine the time when such a possession should pass to the relatives of the deceased, whether immediately after the death of the owner, or not till after the death of the widow who was left behind (*vid.* Num. xxvii. 9 sqq.). No doubt the latter was the rule established by custom, so that the widow remained in possession of the property as long as she lived; and for that length of time she had the right to sell the property in case of need, since the sale of a field was not an actual sale of the field itself, but simply of the yearly produce until the year of Jubilee. Consequently the field of the deceased Elimelech would, strictly speaking, have belonged to his sons, and after their death to Mahlon's widow, since Chilion's widow had remained behind in her own country Moab. But as Elimelech had not only emigrated with his wife and children and died abroad, but his sons had also been with him in the foreign land, and had married and died there, the landed property of their father had not descended to them, but had remained the property of Naomi, Elimelech's widow, in which Ruth, as the widow of the deceased Mahlon, also had a share. Now, in case a widow sold the field of her deceased husband for the time that it was in her possession, on account of poverty, and a relation of her husband redeemed it, it was evidently his duty not only to care for the maintenance of the impoverished widow, but if she were still young, to marry her, and to let the first son born of such a marriage enter into the family of the deceased husband of his wife, so as to inherit the redeemed property, and perpetuate the name and possession of the deceased in Israel. Upon this right, which was founded upon traditional custom, Boaz based this condition, which he set before the nearer redeemer, that if he redeemed the field of Naomi he must also take Ruth, with the obligation to marry her, and through this marriage to set up the name of the deceased upon his inheritance" (pp. 488–90).

28. *'Aḥînû*, although translated "brother" (v. 3), has the extended meaning of "relative" or "kinsman" (i.e., someone from the same extended family), and may have even been used of people who were not related (2 Sam. 1:26) or who had entered into a special covenant (Amos 1:9).
29. KD, 4:490.
30. Cox, p. 141.
31. Watson, p. 413.

Chapter 8

1. Robert Wilder, *Flamingo Road* (New York: Grosset and Dunlap, 1942).
2. See C. J. Barber, "Restoring God's Image in Man," *Theological Students Fellowship Bulletin* 71 (1975), pp. 17–20.
3. William Gesenius, *Hebrew and Chaldee Lexicon to the Old Testament Scriptures*, trans. S. P. Tregelles (Grand Rapids, Mich.: Eerdmans, 1949), p. 293.
4. See C. C. Ryrie, *The Grace of God* (Chicago: Moody, 1963); cf. also R. M. Hals, *Grace and Faith in the Old Testament* (Philadelphia: Fortress, 1980).
5. G. A. Cooke, *Ruth*, was most certainly in error when he stated, "When *property was transferred*, as in the present case, to take off the sandal and hand it to the person in whose favour the transfer is made, gave a symbolic attestation to the act and invested it with legal validity" (pp. 16–17, italics in the original). The unnamed kinsman transferred his rights to Boaz, not to the property. The property had not yet been purchased from Naomi.
6. The word *leqayyēm*, "to confirm," is thought to be an Aramaism (see Joüon, *Ruth*, p. 85). Myers (p. 19), however, pointed out that several middle weak forms are found in the *Piel* as early documents. See also Campbell (p. 148) and Sasson (p. 142).
7. The statements *šālap 'îš na'alô*, "a man would draw off his sandal" (v. 7) and *wayyišlōp na'alô*, "and he drew off his sandal" (v. 8) are worthy of close consideration. Morris has reminded us that some Greek versions (LXX and Aquila) add, "and gave it [the sandal] to him [Boaz]" (p. 308). However, the question is not resolved that easily. Some commen-

tators believed that it was Boaz who gave away his shoe; others held to the theory that they exchanged footwear. Joüon, *Ruth* (p. 88), believed that something had fallen out of the text through transmission. Campbell (p. 149) and Rudolph (p. 60) offered suggestions for this scribal omission. It seems preferable to conclude on the basis of Deuteronomy 25:9 that Boaz was the recipient of his relative's shoe.

8. The word *te'ûdāh*, "attestation, witness," is rare, occurring only here and in Isaiah 8:16, 20. Its meaning in Ruth differs from its usage in Isaiah. For an explanation of its etymology, see Campbell (p. 149) and Sasson (p. 146). Morris said, "The custom is described simply. To confirm whatever was agreed upon, one man drew off (the tense is perfect; one might have expected a frequentative imperfect, but the perfect accords with the fact that the action was performed once only in each case) his sandal and gave it to the other. It is a curious custom, but at least its unusualness would mean that it attracted attention, and this probably was its object" (p. 306).

9. See deVaux, pp. 22, 169; and C. M. Carmichael, "A Ceremonial Crux: Removing a Man's Sandal as a Female Gesture of Contempt," *JBL* 96 (1977), pp. 321–26.

10. Watson asked, "In buying the field and adding it to his estate will the man take Ruth to wife, to raise up the name of the dead upon his inheritance? He is not prepared to do that, for the children of Ruth would be entitled to the portion of ground, and he is unwilling to impoverish his own family" (p. 415).

11. See Taylor, p. 85. Overlooked by most commentators is the fact that this unnamed kinsman was ignorant of Naomi's plight. He was unaware of the fact that her poverty was compelling her to sell the land she and Elimelech at one time had worked together.

12. Morison, p. 62; also Morris, p. 306.

13. The Hebrew was only the word *'ēdîm*, "witnesses." See G. M. Tucker, "Witnesses and 'Dates' in Israelite Contracts," *CBQ* 28 (1966), pp. 42–45.

14. On Boaz's remarks (v. 9), see T. and D. Thompson, "Some Legal Problems in the Book of Ruth," *VT* 18 (1968), pp. 79–99; Sasson, p. 144.

15. Boaz's emphasis is clear. *'Et-rût hammō'abiyyāh 'ēšet maḥlôn qānîtî lî le'iššāh*, "and Ruth the Moabitess, the wife of Mahlon, I have acquired for myself for my wife." Ruth stands first in the sentence for emphasis. And here for the last time she is mentioned as "the Moabitess." From now on the people of Bethlehem would refer to her as "Ruth the wife of Boaz."

16. See Campbell, pp. 151–52.

17. G. A. F. Knight, *Ruth and Jonah* (1966), p. 37.

18. See S. P. Parker, "The Marriage Blessing in Israelite and Ugaritic Literature," *JBL* 95 (1976), pp. 23–30.
19. The perfect tense is used for something that has not yet taken place. This is not uncommon in Hebrew. See Campbell, pp. 152–53.
20. Such a comment was most gracious, and to be bestowed upon a foreigner was most unusual. Note Genesis 29:35 and the comments of Sasson, p. 154.
21. See Campbell, p. 152.
22. See Sasson, pp. 154, 156.
23. See Morris, p. 311.
24. The reference to Ruth as *na'arāh*, "young woman," was translated by Campbell (p. 154) as "young girl" in an endeavor to prove the difference in age between Ruth and Boaz. Whatever difference in age may be implied by the word, it reflected the span of years separating the elders of the city and Ruth. Being the grey-haired, venerable men of Bethlehem, they doubtless saw Ruth as being very young.
25. See J. Hastings, *Encyclopedia of Religion and Ethics* (Edinburgh: T. & T. Clark, 1908), 4:367ff.
26. *TWOT*, 1:132.
27. See J. D. Pentecost, *Things to Come* (Grand Rapids: Zondervan, 1964), pp. 433–55, for an explanation of the theocracy and the ability of God's theocratic representatives to pronounce blessing on someone.
28. KD, p. 491.
29. A euphemism for sexual intercourse.
30. Morris, p. 312.
31. *Ibid.*
32. This conclusion was also reached by P. Humbert, "Art et leçon de l'historie de Ruth, *Opuscules d'un Hebraïsant* (1958), who affirmed that after considering all the events which took place in this book, "the chief actor is God" (p. 108).
33. Taylor, p. 91.

Chapter 9

1. The term was coined by L. Penning and was the title of his 1954 (English translation) biography of the Genevan Reformer.
2. See P. Schaff, *History of the Christian Church* (Grand Rapids: Eerdmans, 1960), 8:360–61. (The quotation we have used comes from a sermon by C. H. Spurgeon.)
3. For an explanation of the covenant, see J. D. Pentecost, *Things to Come*, pp. 65–128.
4. *Ibid.*, pp. 456–63.

5. The interim form of the Kingdom was explained in the parables of Matthew 13. See Pentecost, pp. 138–55; and R. C. Stedman, *Behind History* (Waco, Tex.: Word, 1976), pp. 1–166.

6. The theocracy—one of the most important and least understood aspects of God's revelation—has been treated by Pentecost in *Things to Come*, pp. 433–511.

7. C. P. B. Weiss, *Biblical Theology of the New Testament*, trans. D. Eaton (Edinburgh: T. & T. Clark, 1885), 1:144.

8. Evidence of God's grace is found in the way Ruth was described by the writer. *Wattehî-lô le'iššâ*, "and she [Ruth] became to him [Boaz] a wife" (4:13). The emphasis of the sentence was placed on the word "wife." As we trace the writer's terms used to describe Ruth, we find that she passed from a *nokriyyāh*, "stranger" (2:10), to *šiphāt*, "handmaid" (2:13), to *iššāh*, "wife" (4:13). Sasson (p. 161) pointed out that she was worthy enough to marry a *gibbôr hayil* ("a mighty [man] of valor") of Boaz's stature, becoming his *wife* and not merely his concubine or a handmaiden.

9. The question arises, Who is this *gō'ēl*, "kinsman," Boaz or Obed? Sasson (p. 163) conjectured that after the birth of his son, Boaz was no longer regarded as the *gō'ēl*, and that technically the responsibility for Naomi's support fell on Obed. See Morris, p. 313. However, it is difficult to think of an infant assuming the support of his grandmother, unless the reference here was to position as opposed to performance (i.e., the assuming of a de jure responsibility with Boaz still performing the role of a de facto *gō'ēl*). See J. Bewer, "The Goel in Ruth 4:14, 15," *AJSL* 20 (1903–4), pp. 202–6; Leggett, p. 255-65; Rudolph, p. 69.

10. *Weyiqqārē' šemô beyiśrā'ēl*, "and may his name be called in Israel," conveys the idea of the development of a good reputation. For further comments, see Campbell, p. 163. Joüon, *Ruth* (p. 93), suggested that it was Naomi's husband, Elimelech, who is being referred to. In view of the emphasis of this verse, as well as the one following, it seems as if Obed was the one referred to.

11. The Hebrew *wehāyâ lāk lemēšîb nepeš*, "a restorer of life" (there is no "your" in the Masoretic text as in the KJV), probably referred to the comfort and consolation Obed will bring to Naomi. God, in his grace, would have recompensed her for the loss of her sons. Campbell stated, "Most noteworthy here is that the story-teller picks up the dominant key of the first chapter, *šwb*, 'to return,' especially as it is used in 1:21: 'empty Yahweh has brought me back' (or, 'caused me to return'). The signal is given: Naomi's complaint, dormant since 1:20–21, is here resolved" (p. 164).

12. *Kî kallātēk 'ašer-'ahēbatek yelādattû*, "for your daughter-in-law, who loves you, has borne him," is of interest philologically as well as theo-

logically. After *kî* one expects the verb before the subject. Here the subject comes first, probably for the sake of added emphasis. Sasson (p. 167) offered an explanation that he hoped would resolve the tension between the supposed "two-fold etiological narrative" that had been combined into the story of the "Birth of Obed." His comments were unconvincing and based on the presumption of two sources for the information. Joüon, *Ruth* (p. 94), escaped the problems of the text by changing *ahēbatek*, to *'ahēbātek.* Theologically, we see God's grace at work, for Ruth, a foreigner, succeeded in providing Naomi with an heir to Elimelech's (and Mahlon's) estate. This is something Naomi deemed to be impossible (cf. 1:11–12).

13. The women's praise of Ruth, *'ašer-hî' ṭôbāh lāk miššib'āh bānîm*, "who is better to you than seven sons," should be compared with Job's restoration of his children in 42:10–17.

14. The debate over *wattešitēhû beḥēyqāh*, "and laid him in her bosom," seems incapable of solution. Central in the discussion is whether this was merely an act of affection (cf. 1 Kings 3:20) or a legal sign of adoption. The Hebrew words for breast, or bosom, are varied and colorful. They are used of men as well as women (cf. 2 Sam. 12:3); and, as Campbell (p. 165) reminded us, are employed of "God's shepherding his lambs" (Isa. 40:11).

Yet the NASB translates *ḥêq*, "lap." (For an explanation of Israel's adoption procedures, see Z. Falk, *Hebrew Law in Bible Times*, pp. 163f.; E. Neufeld, *Ancient Hebrew Marriage Laws*, p. 126, n. 1; deVaux, p. 51; Rudolph, pp. 70–71.) A possible solution for this rendering of the Hebrew *ḥêq* may be found in the article by H. A. Hoffner, Jr., "Birth and Name-Giving in Hittite Texts," *JNES* 27 (1968), pp. 198–203. He showed that the placing of a child on the knee was equivalent to conferring on him official recognition and legitimization. Joüon, *Ruth* (p. 94), however, saw no reason for Naomi to adopt (or legitimize) a child considered to be Mahlon's and who will inherit his estate. Gerleman (p. 37) advanced the theory that Naomi's act is a "special type of adoption." However, he failed to provide any convincing proof.

Other commentators, such as Morris (p. 314), Campbell (pp. 164–65), and Rudolph (p. 71), all saw Naomi taking Obed to her heart and loving him as if he were her own. The rendering of *ḥêq* as "breast, bosom" is not only consistent with its use elsewhere, but seems to fit the context here as well. Naomi, in effect, became Obed's "nanny" or "governess."

15. The naming of Ruth's child is a further irregularity in the established procedures of Hebrew life and culture. The fact that the women from the homes near Boaz's gave Obed his name was unusual and finds a parallel only in Luke 1:58–59. Sasson (p. 172) appropriately drew atten-

tion to the fact that these are *šekēnôt*, "neighborhood women," not *našîm*, "women of the city."

This brings up the issue of the child's name, for O. Eissfeldt, *The Old Testament, An Introduction* (1965), pp. 479–480, has pointed out that if *wattiqre'nāh lô haššekēnôt šēm lē'mōr*, "and the neighborhood women gave him a name, saying, . . ." is indeed a formula used at name-giving ceremonies, then the actual name should precede the explanation, *yullad-bēn leno'omî*, "a son has been born to Naomi." He suggests that the name given the child is really *Ben-nā'omî*, "son of Naomi," and that this is taken from the text and Obed (meaning "servant") inserted. See D. R. Ap-Thomas, "The Book of Ruth," *ET* 79 (1968), pp. 369–73; A. Key, "The Giving of Proper Names in the Old Testament," *JBL*, 83 (1918), p. 18, conjectured that the name Obed may be a shortened form of Obadiah. See also Campbell (pp. 166f.), Morris (p. 315), and Sasson (p. 176-78) for a full discussion of this issue.

16. Cox, pp. 143–44.
17. Morris, p. 314.
18. *Ibid.* See also R. J. Sklba, "The Redeemer of Israel," *CBQ* 34 (1972), pp. 13–17.
19. M. D. Johnson, *The Purpose of Biblical Genealogies* (Cambridge: Cambridge U., 1969), p. 52; see also T. C. Mitchell and A. R. Millard, "Genealogy," *IBD*, 1:546ff. Other children born to Boaz and Ruth would have been counted as theirs. The Book of Ruth, however, concentrated solely on the circumstances surrounding the family of Elimelech and "God's steadfast love to the living and the dead" (2:20).
20. KD, 4:493.
21. *Ibid.*
22. *IBD*, 1:546.
23. Morris, p. 317.
24. C. H. Spurgeon, *Gospel of the Kingdom* (Grand Rapids, Mich.: Zondervan, n.d.), pp. 1–2.
25. We should avoid the error made by numerous commentators of presuming that, at the time of the writer, David was king. He became king, but the text of Ruth does not mention him as such. If the book was written by Samuel (as indeed it might have been), Samuel would have known of David's anointing (1 Sam. 16), but would have died before David ascended the throne.

Critical Studies

1. Although the Talmud did not come into existence until the Tannaic period (A.D. 200–500), it did serve as a "hedge" about the sacred writ-

ings of the Jews and sought to preserve their ancient heritage—a heritage that some Jews claim was current as far back as the eighth century B.C. (See Josephus, *Antiquities of the Jews* XIII, 297). Baba Bathra 14b reads: "Samuel wrote the book which bears his name and the Book [note the use of the singular] of Judges and Ruth" (*Babylonian Talmud*, XI:71).

2. KD, 4:466.

3. Negative biblical criticism assigned the writing of the Book of Deuteronomy to the reign of Josiah (622 B.C.). Not being prepared to yield their presupposition to evidence to the contrary, those who espouse the late date for the writing of Deuteronomy feel compelled to date the Book of Ruth (1) after the time of Josiah, (2) during the Babylonian exile, or (3) in the postexilic period of Ezra-Nehemiah, for the contents of Ruth gives evidence of a knowledge of Deuteronomy. For a helpful discussion of the dating of Deuteronomy, see Archer, pp. 251–62.

4. Certain words, supposedly of Aramaic origin or characteristic of later Hebrew, are frequently cited as proof of the late date of Ruth: e.g., *nāśā nāśîm*, "they took wives" (1:4); *lāhēn*, "for them" (1:13); *'āgan*, "endure" (1:13); *mārā'*, "bitter" (1:20); *'ānâh be*, "has eyed me" (1:21); *miqreh*, "chance" (2:3); *ta'abûrî*, "leave" (2:8); *yiqṣôrûn*, "harvest" (2:9); *tidbāqîn*, "stay close" (2:21); *yāradty*, "go down" (3:3); *šākābty*, "lie down" (3:4); *ta' aśîn*, "to do" (3:4); *margēlōt*, "feet"(?) (3:7, 8, 14); *tēde'in*, "shall know" (3:18); *pelōnî'almōnî*, "such a one"(?) (4:1); *qayyēm*, "confirm" (4:7); *šālap na'alô*, "draw off . . . his sandal" (4:7). See L. P. Smith, "The Book of Ruth," *Interpreter's Bible*, (Nashville: Abingdon, 1956), 2:830. Morris (p. 233), however, quotes D. J. Wiseman of the British Museum as affirming that these words "are now known from the Middle Babylonian and Middle Assyrian period, c. 1400 B.C."

5. See C. F. Keil, *Lehrbuch der Historisch-kritischen Einleitung in die Schriften des Alten Testaments* (Leipzig: J. C. Mohr, 1873), p. 437. Harrison said, "The direct character of the narrative seems to imply that David had not yet become the legendary personage of Israel" (p. 1061). With this E. J. Young, *An Introduction to the Old Testament* (Grand Rapids: Eerdmans, 1949), p. 330, was in essential agreement.

6. These include (roughly in accordance with the date assigned the book by each writer) Wright, p. xliv, with which compare his later *Introduction to the Old Testament* (New York: T. Whitaker, 1890), p. 126; Driver, pp. 454ff.; Hertzberg, p. 257; Rudolph, p. 29; F. W. Albright, "Ruth," in H. C. Alleman and E. E. Flack, *Old Testament Commentary* (Philadelphia: Fortress, 1954), p. 147; R. Hals, *The Theology of the Book of Ruth* (Philadelphia: Fortress, 1969), p. 73; G. von Rad, *Old Testament Theology* (Philadelphia: Westminster, 1962), 1:52; W. W. Cannon, "The Book of Ruth," *Theology* 16 (1928), p. 315; and S. Davidson, *Intro-*

duction to the Old Testament (Edinburgh: T. & T. Clark, 1862), 1:482ff.

7. G. H. A. von Ewald, *Geschichte des Volkes Israel* (Göttingen: Dietericht, 1864), p. 225; E. König, *Einleitung in das Alte Testament* (Leipzig: J. C. Hinrichs, 1893), p. 287; Sasson, p. 244.

8. Cf. O. Eissfeldt, *The Old Testament: An Introduction* (Philadelphia: Westminster, 1965), p. 483; G. Fohrer, *Introduction to the Old Testament* (London: S.P.C.K., 1970), pp. 251–52; Gray, pp. 398–400; Joüon, *Ruth*, pp. 12ff.; W. O. E. Oesterley and T. H. Robinson, *Introduction to the Books of the Old Testament* (Oxford, Clarendon, 1950), p. 150; D. R. Ap-Thomas, "The Book of Ruth," *ET* 79 (1968), pp. 369–73; see also B. S. Childs, *Introduction to the Old Testament as Scripture* (Philadelphia: Fortress, 1979), where he made a claim that the writer of Ruth "drew material from I Chronicles 2 in order to confirm the testimony" (p. 567). However, might not the writer of Chronicles have taken his material from the Book of Ruth? Archer (pp. 105–18, 251–62) and Harrison (pp. 495–541, 635–62) argued convincingly for an early date of Deuteronomy.

9. C. Cornill, *Introduction to the Canonical Books of the Old Testament* (New York: G. P. Putnam's Sons, 1907), p. 255.

10. Myers, pp. 19ff. The archaic forms are thought to be *tidbāqîn*, "stay" (2:8, 21); *yiqṣōrûn*, "harvest" (2:9); *yiš'abûn*, "draw" (2:9); *weyāradty*, "and go down" (3:3); *wešākābty*, "and lie down" (3:4); *ta'aśîn*, "you are to do" (3:4); *tēde'în*, "you shall know" (3:18); *qenôtekā*, "you buy, acquire" (4:5). Myers, however, did not believe that the Book of Ruth went through a two-fold form of transmission. See also G. Glanzman, "The Origin and Date of the Book of Ruth," *CBQ* 21 (1959), 201–7; and M. Crook, "The Book of Ruth," *JBL* 16 (1948), pp. 155f.

11. Gerleman, 18:7–8.

12. J. J. Davis, *Conquest and Crisis* (Grand Rapids: Baker, 1969), p. 156; and L. J. Wood, *Distressing Days of the Judges* (Grand Rapids: Zondervan, 1975), p. 254.

13. S. M. Zwemer, *Sons of Adam* (Grand Rapids: Baker, 1951), p. 17; see also J. Coppens, *The Old Testament and Its Critics*, trans. E. A. Ryan and E. W. Tribbe (Patterson, N.J.: St. Anthony Guild Press, 1942), p. 75.

14. W. S. Churchill, "Moses: The Leader of a People," *Sunday Chronicle*, 8 November 1931, p. 7.

15. Cornill (pp. 464f.) believed that *kanōn* was a "Semitic loan-word" that the early Greeks adopted and adapted. He cited illustrations from Greek literature to show *kanōn* originally meant "wood" (similar to the Semitic *kaneh*, "reed." See Homer, *The Iliad*, viii, 193; xiii, 407; and xxiii, 761). He then referred his readers to the usage of the word by Ezekiel (40:3), where it had come to mean "the rule of the carpenter." In later Greek writing *kanōn* acquired the sense of "norm, rule, standard."

16. *Mishnah*, Yadim, 3:2; 4:5 (see H. Danby's translation, pp. 781, 784).
17. Flavius Josephus, "Contra Apion," *The Works of Josephus* (1926), 1:8.
18. See P. Katz, *Zeitschrift für die Neutestamentliche Wissenschaft* 47 (1956), pp. 199–201.
19. See the conclusions of the brilliant Semitic scholar R. Laird Harris in *Inspiration and Canonicity of the Bible* (Chicago: Moody, 1957), 304 pp.; "Was the Law and the Prophets Two-Thirds of the Canon?" *Bulletin of the Evangelical Theological Society* 9 (1966), pp. 163–71; and "Canon," *ZPEB*, 1:709–31, in which Harris argued persuasively for a twofold division of the Old Testament.
20. Cf., H. B. Swete, *An Introduction to the Old Testament in Greek* (New York: Ktav, 1968), pp. 197–264.
21. According to W. Smith and H. Wace, *A Dictionary of Christian Biography* (London: John Murray, 1882), "Melito, bishop of Sardis, the capital of Lydia, held, in the third quarter of the 2nd century, a foremost place among the bishops of Asia, both in respect of personal influence and literary activity" (4:894). Eusebius of Pamphylia, in his *Historia Ecclesiasticus*, quoted from a letter written by Melito in which he referred to a visit to Palestine where he diligently ascertained "the accurate facts about their writings, how many they are in number, and what is their order" (iv. 26. 13f.). In the list provided by Melito, Ruth came immediately after Judges.
22. J. P. Audet, "A Hebrew-Aramaic List of Books of the Old Testament in Greek Transcription," *JTS*, New Series, 1 (1950), pp. 135–54.
23. The "Writings" or *Hagiographa* included Psalms, Proverbs, Job, Daniel, Ezra-Nehemiah (counted as one book), 1 and 2 Chronicles (also counted as one book), and the five *Megilloth*, or rolls, used at separate festivals (Song of Solomon at Passover; Ruth at the Feast of Weeks; Lamentations on the ninth of Ab, the anniversary of the Babylonian destruction of the Temple; Ecclesiastes at the Feast of Tabernacles; and Esther at Purim). See also W. W. Cannon, "The Book of Ruth," *Theology* 16 (1928), p. 317.
24. This is the reason Bewer (p. 428) gave for the exclusion of Daniel from the prophetic writings.
25. According to Cornill (pp. 472–80) and Eissfeldt (pp. 565–68) the Pentateuch was written between 950–450 B.C. Because of its notable place in the history of God's ancient people, this portion of the canon was quickly closed. The Prophets, however, took longer to be recognized as authoritative, and this portion of the canon did not close until 200 B.C. The third stage, the canonization of the Writings, did not come until A.D. 90 when, following the destruction of the Temple and the dispersion of the Jews, some authoritative listing of the writings they held

sacred was at last made. See A. Spanier's article "Canon," *Universal Jewish Encyclopedia* (New York: Universal Jewish Encyclopedia, 1941), 3:12. Such theories we find untenable.

26. J. P. Lewis, "What Do We Mean by Jamnia?" *JBR* 32 (1964), pp. 125–32.

27. *Introductory Guide to the Old Testament* (Grand Rapids: Zondervan, 1951), pp. 126–27; see also Harrison, p. 278, and Archer, pp. 66–72.

28. W. E. Staples, "The Book of Ruth," *AJSL* 53 (1937), pp. 145ff.; L. P. Smith, *Interpreter's Bible*, 2:830; H. May, "Ruth's Visit to the High Place at Bethlehem," *JRAS* 75 (1939), pp. 75–78; and S. Shearman and J. Curtis, "Divine-Human Conflicts in the Old Testament, *JNES* 28 (1969), pp. 235–40. Eissfeldt says: "Staples' view that all the names which appear in the book have reference to the fertility cult is no more probable than his assertion that the book, which in his view reveals many other motifs belonging to this cult, is intended to depict the transition from sorrow to joy in the course of the world's life, and to present the birth of a child as the sign of a more fortunate age" (p. 481).

29. "The Theme of the Ruth Story," *CBQ* 22 (1960), p. 391.

30. R. G. Moulton, *The Modern Reader's Bible* (New York: Macmillan, 1937), pp. 1375–76; see also W. McKane, *Tracts for the Times: Ruth, Esther, Lamentations, Ecclesiastes, Song of Songs* (London: SCM, 1965), p. 12; S. Bertram, "Symmetrical Design in the Book of Ruth," *JBL* 84 (1965), pp. 165–68; and D. Rauber, "Literary Values in Ruth," *JBL* 89 (1970), pp. 27–37.

31. Sasson, p. 197. W. F. Albright, however, pointed out that "the Israelites had developed a previously unknown type of narrative style, simple and direct, equally suited for recounting tales and for recounting historical episodes. . . . The delicacy of the story of Ruth remains unsurpassed anywhere; Ruth's loyalty to her mother-in-law, the scene between her and Boaz in chapter three, and the final episode with Naomi (4:14–17) are gems of world literature" (*Archaeology and the Religion of Israel* [Baltimore: Johns Hopkins U., 1953], pp. 22–23).

32. Driver, p. 456.

33. Eissfeldt, pp. 480ff.; and a reply, "The Plot of the Book of Ruth," *BJRL* 32 (1950), pp. 207–28.

34. J. Titterington, "A Case Study in Friendship," *His* (January 1976), pp. 1, 4ff.; *Interpreter's Bible*, (Nashville: Abingdon), 2:831; R. G. Moulton, *Biblical Idyls* (Boston: D. C. Heath, 1896), p. xxvi.

35. J. Hempel, *Das Ethos des Alten Testaments* (Berlin: A Töpelmann, 1938), p. 172.

36. I. Bettan, *The Five Scrolls* (Cincinnati: Union of American Hebrew Congregations), p. 53.

37. L. Ryken, *Literature of the Bible* (Grand Rapids: Zondervan, 1974), p. 72.

38. KD, 4:466.

39. G. Campbell Morgan, *Living Messages of the Books of the Bible* (Old Tappan, N.J.: Revell, 1912), pp. 134–36.

40. *Ibid.*, pp. 136–37.

41. KD, 4:466.

42. Fuerst, p. 5; cf. also Eissfeldt, p. 479; E. Selin, *Introduction to the Old Testament*, p. 250; Driver, pp. 455f.; W. R. Smith, "The Book of Ruth," *Encyclopedia Biblica* (London: A. and C. Black, 1907), 4: col. 4169; Joüon, *Ruth*, p. 96; and many others.

43. A. Jepsen, "Das Buch Ruth," *Theologische Studien und Kritiken* 108 (1937–1938), pp. 416–28, believed that the book was written during the exilic period. He said: "And when it is now recorded how, contrary to despair and despondency, a new heir is presented to Naomi, this was for the exiled in their despondency a word which comforted them and filled them with new courage. So it cannot be denied that the book of Ruth, with this interpretation, is understandable especially in the time of the exile.

    "Israel had, as the childless barren widow, as the deserted wife, nothing to expect from the future, just like the widow Naomi, who was robbed of her children."

44. R. Hals, *The Theology of the Book of Ruth* (1969), p. 75. By way of contrast, Sasson (p. 232) believed that the book was written at a time when the Davidic dynasty was almost extinct. Its composition was intended to bolster David's claim to the throne.

45. See C. J. Barber, *Nehemiah and the Dynamics of Effective Leadership* (Neptune, N.J.: Loizeaux, 1976), pp. 121–47. Not to be overlooked in this discussion is the spiritual awakening of chapters 8–10 and the signing of a covenant by the people pledging their loyalty to the Word of the Lord. See also W. R. Eichhorst, "Ezra's Ethics on Intermarriage and Divorce," *Grace Journal* 10 (Fall 1969), pp. 16–28.

46. Those favoring the view that Ruth is a polemic against Ezra and Nehemiah include R. H. Pfeiffer, *Introduction to the Old Testament* (1941), pp. 717ff. and G. A. F. Knight, *Ruth and Jonah* (1966), pp. 15–23.

47. Margaret B. Crook, "The Book of Ruth," *JBR* 16 (1948), pp. 155–60.

48. S. Davidson, 1:482ff.; cf. Wright, *Introduction to the Old Testament*, p. 126; Young, p. 339.

49. B. Vellas, "The Book of Ruth and Its Purpose," *Theologia Athens* (1954), pp. 7ff.; see also G. A. Cooke, *The Book of Ruth* (Cambridge: Cambridge U., 1918), p. xiii; Hertzberg, p. 258; H. H. Rowley, *Growth of the Old Testament*, p. 151; and "The Marriage of Ruth," *HTR* 40 (1947), p. 78.

50. L. Finkelstein, *The Pharisees* (New York: Ktav, 1938), 2:540; see also the *Talmud*, Yebamoth, 47b; *Midrash Rabbah*, Ruth 2:22–24.

51. D. Harvey, "Ruth, Book of," *Interpreter's Dictionary of the Bible*, 4:133.

52. Vellas, pp. 10ff. See also H. Bronkers, "Enkele Opmerkingen over Het

Verband Tussen Lessing en Leviraat in Ruth IV," *Nederlands The-ologisch Tijdschrift* 2 (1947–48), pp. 2–7.

53. J. P. Hyatt, "Ruth, Book of," *HDB* (1902), p. 865. Bronkers, cited above, said: "A careful study of the content of this chapter can lead to no other conclusion than that the author here attempts to make acceptable that under certain circumstances the concept of redemption ought to in-clude the obligation to levirate marriage even in its most extensive form. An extension of the obligation to redeem is propagated here, an extension which, according to the author, always existed in earlier times but which in his day had fallen into disuse" (p. 4). See also E. Neufeld, *The Hittite Laws* (London: Luzac and Co., 1951), p. 192; and G. R. Driver and J. C. Miles, *The Assyrian Laws* (Oxford: Clarendon, 1935), p. 242. These all support, on philological and historical grounds, a widening of the levirate marriage custom.
54. Rowley, "The Marriage of Ruth," *HTR* 40 (1947), p. 171. See also M. Burrows, "Levirate Marriage in Israel," *JBL* 59 (1940), pp. 23–33; "The Ancient Oriental Background of Hebrew Levirate Marriage," *BASOR* 77 (1940), pp. 2–15; and E. Neufeld, *Ancient Hebrew Marriage Laws* (Lon-don: Longmans, Green, 1944), pp. 23–55.
55. S. R. Driver, *Critical and Exegetical Commentary on Deuteronomy* (Edinburgh: T. & T. Clark, 1896), p. 285. Cf. L. M. Epstein's claim that a sharp distinction existed between levirate and *ge'ullah* marriage, *Mar-riage Laws in the Bible and the Talmud* (Cambridge, Mass.: Harvard U., 1942), pp. 86–89. This distinction was held by many competent scholars.
56. This concept was fleshed out by D. F. Rauber, "Literary Values in the Bible: The Book of Ruth," *JBL* 89 (1970), pp. 27–37.
57. O. Loretz, "The Theme of the Ruth Story," *CBQ* 22 (1960), pp. 391–99.
58. *Das Buch Ruth*, p. 32.
59. *Ruth*, p. 242.
60. Rudolph said: "Certainly the narrator exercises all care in the portrayal of the individual characters. . . . That Ruth arrives at the right field, however, is Yahweh's leading; that the clever plan of Naomi comes to fruition is Yahweh's mercy; and that the desired son is produced from the marriage with Boaz is Yahweh's gift" (p. 32).
61. A. Jepsen, "Das Buch Ruth," *Theologische Studien und Kritiken* 108 (1937–38), p. 423.
62. *Ruth*, p. 242.
63. KD, 4:466.

SCRIPTURE INDEX

PERSON and TITLE INDEX